CRUCIAL TRUTHS IN THE HOLY SCRIPTURES

VOLUME 2

WITNESS LEE

Living Stream Ministry

Anaheim, CA · www.lsm.org

First Edition, June 2008.

ISBN 978-0-7363-3517-1

Published by

Living Stream Ministry
2431 W. La Palma Ave., Anaheim, CA 92801 U.S.A.
P. O. Box 2121, Anaheim, CA 92814 U.S.A.

Printed in the United States of America

17   18   19   20   21   22   /   9   8   7   6   5   4   3   2

CONTENTS

PREFACE

Crucial Truths in the Holy Scriptures was originally published in Chinese as a six-volume set containing sixty topics of basic truths in the Bible. The topics and verses were selected and arranged by Witness Lee, and these books were greatly used by the Lord in the early spread of the local churches throughout the Far East. Volume 2 contains topics 17 through 26. Future volumes in English will complete the series. These messages have been translated from Chinese.

PREFACE TO THE CHINESE EDITION

In order for the children of God, especially new believers, to receive a greater supply of the Word, we, by the Lord's grace, wish to present some crucial truths in the Holy Scriptures so that the children of God may receive a foundation in the Word of God.

These crucial truths, originally presented as forty-two topics, were studied by Witness Lee with the brothers and sisters in Chefoo. Later, in the autumn of 1949, Brother Lee studied them again with the brothers and sisters in Taipei and added eighteen topics for a total of sixty topics in all. Chapters 1 through 16 cover the condition of a sinner to the time of knowing his salvation. Chapters 17 through 60 examine various matters a believer should know and pursue after his salvation, with chapters 17 through 26 specifically covering ten matters a believer should practice after his salvation.

The purpose of these crucial truths is to make the matters of the Lord's salvation clear to those who lack an understanding of their salvation. Furthermore, they lay a foundation in the various aspects of fundamental biblical truths for believers who are clear about their salvation. The purpose is specific, but the messages are diverse.

The notes on these crucial truths contain much light that is precious and urgently needed by the children of God. We look to the Lord to inspire every brother and sister to read and study these notes carefully. We believe this will enable them not only to receive a foundation in the Word of God but also to receive manifold help in knowing the Bible.

The Editorial Section
Taiwan Gospel Book Room

CHAPTER SEVENTEEN

BAPTISM

I. The importance of baptism.
II. The relationship between baptism and salvation.
III. The meaning of baptism:
    A. Into Christ.
    B. Into Christ's death to be buried and raised together with Him.
    C. The testimony of a good conscience.
IV. The meaning of the word *baptism*.
V. The pattern of baptism.
VI. The type of baptism.
VII. The ones being baptized.
VIII. The one baptizing.
IX. The time of baptism.
X. The place of baptism.
XI. The correction of baptism.

In the first sixteen topics, we saw the aspects of God's salvation. Now we will study matters that one must practice after being saved. The first of these concerns baptism.

God's interaction with man and the service He requires of man can be divided into the age of the Old Testament and the age of the New Testament. The former is a type of the latter. Thus, the former is a shadow and prefigure, and the latter is the reality, the body of the shadow. In the Old Testament age of shadows and prefigures, service was a matter of rituals and ordinances; in the New Testament age of truth and reality, service is a matter of spirit and life. Nevertheless, in the New Testament age there are at least four matters that God wants man to practice, which from their outward appearance seem to be rituals and ordinances. These four matters are baptism, the laying on of hands, head covering, and the breaking of bread. Although God abolished the rituals and ordinances of the Old Testament and requires man to serve Him in spirit and reality in the New Testament, He requires man to practice four matters that seem to be rituals and ordinances. This proves that these four matters are very important in God's eyes; therefore, we should pay attention to them and not despise them. Actually, they are not matters of ritual and ordinance; rather, they are practical steps and concrete processes through which we receive, obtain, enjoy, and utilize God's salvation and all of its blessings. All that God accomplished and prepared for us in Christ, all that He wants to give us in the new covenant, is dispensed into us through these practical steps and concrete processes. Therefore, if a believer wishes to completely and fully receive and enjoy God's salvation in His Son, he must properly appreciate and practice these steps and processes. The first of these is baptism.

THE IMPORTANCE OF BAPTISM

1. "The baptism which John proclaimed" (Acts 10:37; see also Luke 3:3).

At the beginning of the New Testament age, the first thing God did was to send John the Baptist to proclaim baptism. John was the first servant sent by God at the beginning of the

New Testament, and the baptism preached by him was God's first message in the New Testament. This shows the importance of baptism in God's plan and arrangement. We can say that baptism began the New Testament. Just as the teaching of baptism was God's way of beginning the New Testament age, the practice of baptism is man's way to begin to enjoy the blessings of the New Testament.

2. "It is fitting for us in this way to fulfill all righteousness" (Matt. 3:15).

We see the importance of baptism even more in the fact that the Lord Jesus also needed to be baptized. Although He was the Son of God who came to be our Savior, He still kept God's ordination for men because He was a man. According to His humanity, it was fitting for Him to do this. In doing this, He was a man according to God's procedure. Before God, He fulfilled all righteousness. Since even the Lord as a man needed to be baptized and since it was fitting for Him to fulfill righteousness before God in this way, how much more should we do the same! Since baptism was the fitting way for even the Lord as a man to fulfill all righteousness, we should realize that baptism is extremely important.

3. "The Pharisees and the lawyers rejected the counsel of God for themselves since they had not been baptized by him" (Luke 7:30).

This passage also speaks of the importance of baptism. Baptism is a matter in the counsel, or the plan, of God. If a person is not baptized, he rejects the counsel of God for himself. This is very serious. The Pharisees and lawyers who rejected and opposed the Lord Jesus did this; how can we, who receive the Lord today, be like them in this matter?

4. "Unless one is born of water and the Spirit, he cannot enter into the kingdom of God" (John 3:5).

When we studied regeneration in chapter 11, we saw that *born of water* refers to baptism. Baptism is a necessary step a person must take to enter into the kingdom of God. It is important.

5. "Jesus and His disciples came into the land of Judea, and there He spent some time with them and

baptized"; "Jesus was making and baptizing more disciples than John" (John 3:22; 4:1).

John the Baptist was not the only one who came out to preach and baptize people; the Lord Jesus also baptized people when He began to preach. Not only was He Himself baptized in order to fulfill righteousness before God, but He, through His disciples, baptized people in order to accomplish God's will, to be according to God's procedure, and to fulfill God's righteousness. All these show the importance of baptism.

6. "Go therefore and disciple all the nations, baptizing them into the name of the Father and of the Son and of the Holy Spirit" (Matt. 28:19).

When the Lord Jesus was on the earth, He baptized people through His disciples, and even after His resurrection, He commissioned His disciples to go out into all the inhabited earth to preach the gospel to people and to baptize them. His last command before His ascension shows that baptizing people is an important matter that we must carry out when we preach the gospel to people and when we disciple them. Just as preaching the gospel is important, baptizing is important. To merely preach the gospel to people without baptizing them is not sufficient and does not completely keep the Lord's last command.

7. "He who believes and is baptized shall be saved" (Mark 16:16).

Here the Lord says that baptism is a necessary step in a person's full salvation, proving that baptism is important.

8. "What should we do, brothers? And Peter said to them, Repent and each one of you be baptized upon the name of Jesus Christ for the forgiveness of your sins, and you will receive the gift of the Holy Spirit" (Acts 2:37-38, see also v. 41).

On the day of Pentecost many heard Peter's word and were pricked in their hearts, so they asked Peter what they should do. He told them to repent and be baptized upon the name of Jesus Christ for the forgiveness of their sins and to receive the gift of the Holy Spirit. When they heard his word, they were immediately baptized. This also shows the importance of baptism. Peter's directions emphasize baptism. Peter considered baptism as important as repentance and believing on the name of the Lord. He was not like today's preachers who mostly emphasize repentance and believing on the name of the Lord but neglect baptism. Baptism is related to a person's sins being forgiven and to receiving the Holy Spirit. The first group of people, who turned to the Lord and were added to the church after the Lord ascended into the heavens and poured out the Holy Spirit, were baptized. The first mention of any matter in the Bible is a pattern for that particular matter. According to this principle, the baptism of the first group of people who believed is a pattern for all subsequent believers.

9. "The eunuch said, Look, water. What prevents me from being baptized?" (Acts 8:36).

The Ethiopian eunuch spoke this word to Philip, who had preached the gospel to him. This proves that Philip not only preached the gospel but also baptism. If he had not preached baptism, how could a Gentile, who was from a faraway place and had never heard the gospel, know about baptism? How could he have known that he should be baptized and then request baptism? Philip preached the gospel and baptism simultaneously, proving that he saw the importance of baptism. Therefore, when we preach the gospel to people, we should also speak to them about baptism. Baptism should always follow the gospel. Our gospel preaching should not lead people merely to believe but also to be baptized. Believing is important, and baptism is also important. This is the reason that the Holy Spirit did not immediately carry Philip away, even though he clearly had preached the gospel and baptism to the eunuch. Philip was carried away by the Holy Spirit only after he had baptized the eunuch and the eunuch had come up out of the water. This is strong proof that the Lord considers baptism to be very important. In His view, if we preach the gospel to others and lead them to believe in Him without baptizing them, our work of turning others to Him is not finished. Thus, He waited until after Philip had baptized the eunuch before He acknowledged Philip's work as complete by carrying him away. Since the Lord considers baptism to be so important, how can we ignore it? How can we only preach the gospel without baptizing those who believe? How can we only lead people to the Lord but not baptize them?

10. "And now, why do you delay? Rise up and be baptized and wash away your sins, calling on His name" (Acts 22:16).

This was Ananias's word to the newly saved Saul (who later became Paul). This word shows that the early disciples placed much emphasis on baptism. Ananias knew that Saul had met the Lord on the road to Damascus, that the scales had fallen off his eyes through the laying on of his hands, and that he had received the outpouring of the Holy Spirit (9:17-18), yet Ananias still wanted Paul to be baptized and even hurried him to be baptized. If baptism is not important, and if the disciples did not emphasize baptism, why did Ananias hasten Paul to be baptized?

11. "Can anyone forbid the water so that these would not be baptized, who have received the Holy Spirit even as we? And he charged them to be baptized in the name of Jesus Christ" (Acts 10:47-48).

Although the household of Cornelius visibly received the Holy Spirit, Peter still wanted them to be baptized. Does this not prove that baptism is important? Does this not show how much Peter emphasized baptism? He did not do what many today advocate when they speak of only needing a spiritual baptism, not a water baptism. He said that those who had received the baptism of the Spirit still needed to be baptized in water. Moreover, he baptized them in water because they had received the baptism of the Spirit. In Peter's eyes, being baptized in water and receiving the Spirit were equally important. His view is also the Spirit's view and the Lord's view.

12. "He took them with him in that very hour of the night and washed their wounds. And he was baptized immediately, he and all his household" (Acts 16:33).

When the Philippian jailer and his household received the Lord, Paul and Silas, still wounded from being beaten, immediately baptized them. This tells us that baptism is extremely important. If it were not, why would these two brothers, who had been beaten with rods and who were wounded and exhausted from being in jail, immediately baptize the whole household at that very hour of the night?

13. "When they heard this, they were baptized into the name of the Lord Jesus" (Acts 19:5).

The day Paul came to Ephesus, he asked the disciples what baptism they had received, because he was concerned about the baptism of the Holy Spirit. When he discovered they had received only the baptism of John, he solemnly told them that the baptism of John was over and that people should be baptized into the name of the Lord. When they heard this, they were immediately baptized. Paul did not merely find out with what baptism they had been baptized, but he also told them with what baptism they should be baptized. Although they had received the baptism of John, they were immediately baptized again when they heard about baptism into the Lord's name. This proves that they thought baptism is very important.

THE RELATIONSHIP BETWEEN
BAPTISM AND SALVATION

Many today think and preach that baptism is not related to salvation. This thought is not according to the Bible. The Bible solemnly, definitely, and clearly says that baptism is related to salvation and that the relationship is a direct one.

1. "Unless one is born of water and the Spirit, he cannot enter into the kingdom of God" (John 3:5).

Our Lord said that in order to be regenerated into the kingdom of God, one must be born not only of the Spirit but also of water. When the Lord spoke of being born of water, He was referring to baptism. Thus, baptism causes a person to enter into the kingdom of God; it is a requirement for one's entrance into the kingdom of God. This, of course, does not refer to the outward appearance of baptism but to the reality of baptism. However, we cannot spiritualize the reality and say that we do not need the practice. If a person wants to enter into the kingdom of God, he must repent and believe to receive the Lord's life through the Holy Spirit, and he must also be baptized to terminate everything of himself through the water of baptism.

2. "Rise up and be baptized and wash away your sins, calling on His name"; "Repent and each one of you be baptized upon the name of Jesus Christ for the forgiveness of your sins, and you will receive the gift of the Holy Spirit" (Acts 22:16; 2:38).

The Lord's word in these verses clearly indicates that baptism washes away our sins, causes our sins to be forgiven, and enables us to receive the Holy Spirit. The term *wash away your sins* in the verses above refers to the washing away before others of our sins in our rebellion against God and opposition to the Lord (see the section "Cleansing at the Time of Salvation" in chapter 7). *Forgiveness of your sins* refers to more than the forgiveness of our sins in that aspect. This shows that baptism is related to the forgiveness of our sins; baptism along with repentance and believing on the name of the Lord are requirements for the forgiveness of sins. Furthermore, baptism, repentance, and believing on the Lord's name are also related to receiving the Holy Spirit and are requirements for receiving Him. Therefore, if, before others, we want to be washed of our sins of rebelling against God and opposing the Lord, and if we want our sins to be forgiven and to receive the Holy Spirit, we must not only repent and believe on the Lord's name, but we must also be baptized.

3. "As many of you as were baptized into Christ have put on Christ"; "All of us who have been baptized into Christ Jesus have been baptized into His death"; "Buried together with Him in baptism, in which also you were raised together with Him" (Gal. 3:27; Rom. 6:3; Col. 2:12).

These verses in the Bible show how closely baptism is related to our salvation in Christ. Baptism is the process by which we are put into Christ. It is also the way we are put into His death, are buried together with Him, and are raised together with Him. Through baptism, we are put into Christ and into His death, and we are buried and raised together with Him. Thus, baptism does not *represent* our co-death, co-burial, and co-resurrection with Christ, as is taught by many in today's Christianity; rather, baptism is the *reality* of our entrance into Christ, His death, burial, and resurrection. This requires faith, but our inward heart of faith also requires the outward act of baptism to work together with it. If we want to enter into Christ and into His death and to be buried and raised together with Him, we must have the inward faith and the outward act of baptism.

4. "He who believes and is baptized shall be saved"; "Which water, as the antitype, also now saves you, that is, baptism...through the resurrection of Jesus Christ" (Mark 16:16; 1 Pet. 3:21).

Many say that it is enough to only believe and that we do not need to be baptized. But the Lord said, "He who believes and is baptized shall be saved." According to the Lord's word, if a person wants to be saved, he needs to believe and he also needs to be baptized. Just as believing is a requirement for salvation, baptism is also a requirement for salvation. Therefore, Peter said that baptism saves us.

Many change the Lord's word, which says, "He who believes and is baptized shall be saved," into "he who believes and is saved shall be baptized." They think that believing is a procedure prior to salvation and that baptism comes after being saved. Actually, the Lord means that both procedures, believing and baptism, come before salvation. Although salvation is just one step, it requires the movement of two feet. The first step is believing, and the second step is baptism; both feet together add up to one complete step, or procedure, through which we receive the Lord's complete salvation. There are different parts to the Lord's salvation; some parts are obtained by our faith and some are participated in through our baptism. Faith is the inward aspect by which we inwardly receive the Lord's salvation; baptism is the outward action by which we outwardly apply the Lord's salvation. If we have only faith without baptism, we can receive only one aspect of the Lord's salvation; that is, we will have only a partial salvation and will not utilize or apply all aspects of the Lord's full salvation. If we want to participate in all aspects of the Lord's salvation, if we want to be fully saved, we must believe and be baptized.

THE MEANING OF BAPTISM

Into Christ

1. "Baptized into Christ Jesus" (Rom. 6:3).

In John 3:16 the word *into* follows the word *believes* in the original language. Thus, just as we believe into Christ, so also we are baptized into Christ; both cause us to enter into Christ and to be joined to Him. Just as we are joined to Christ through believing to partake of Him, so we are joined to Him through baptism to partake of Him. Believing and being baptized cause us to enter into Christ and become persons in Christ.

Into Christ's Death to Be Buried and Raised Together with Him

1. "Baptized into His death...buried therefore with Him through baptism into His death"; "Buried together with Him in baptism, in which also you were raised together with Him" (Rom. 6:3-4; Col. 2:12).

Since we are baptized into Christ, we are also baptized into His death. Baptism causes us to be joined to Christ and to participate in His death, burial, and resurrection. Since baptism puts us into Christ, it also puts us into His death to be buried and raised together with Him. Therefore, we, who are baptized into Christ, enter into His death, are buried with Him, and are raised with Him, being completely joined to Him. In His death the old life of the self dies completely, and we die forever to sin and the world; in His burial the self and all our past are completely terminated; in His resurrection we receive His life and have a new beginning of life. Therefore, when we go into the water to be baptized, by faith we enter into Christ's death and allow the self, everything of the self, and everything related to the self to be buried in Christ's burial, in the tomb of the baptismal waters. By faith we then come out of the water and allow Christ to live in us in His resurrection.

Therefore, baptism causes us to be joined to the death, burial, and resurrection of Christ. His death and burial terminate the self and everything related to the self, freeing us from sin and the world. Only death and burial can cause a person to be terminated. No matter how lively or active a person is, once he is dead and buried, everything is finished. Only death and burial can free a person from sin and release a person from the world. Only the dead can be freed from sin, totally cutting off their relationship with sin. Only the dead can be freed from the world and say "goodbye" to the world. Moreover, only a person who is buried can completely leave the world; the world leaves no shadow or trace on a buried one. The functions of death and burial are the negative aspects of the meaning of baptism. In its negative aspect, baptism puts us into Christ's death and burial, freeing us from the self, sin, the world, the things of the old creation, the things of Satan, and everything apart from God. In its positive aspect, baptism joins us to Christ's resurrection. This resurrection causes us to become a new creation, to participate in the divine life in Christ with all its riches, and to enter into the new realm of resurrection where old things have passed away and everything is made new. This is the reality of baptism and the positive aspect of baptism.

The Testimony of a Good Conscience

1. "Baptism, not a putting away of the filth of the flesh but the appeal of a good conscience unto God" (1 Pet. 3:21).

Because baptism puts us into Christ, causing us to be joined to His death, burial, and resurrection, it gives us a good conscience, and from this good conscience, it produces a testimony of the Lord's salvation. In the past we were in our corrupt and sinful selves; consequently, our conscience was not good. Since baptism put us into Christ through the redemption accomplished by His death and the justification caused by His resurrection, our conscience becomes good, and through baptism there is a testimony that we who died, were buried, and are resurrected together with Christ are partakers of Christ. Our sins are forgiven in Him because of His redemption, and we are justified in Him because of His resurrection. Thus, baptism gives us a good conscience through our entering into Christ and our entering into His death, burial, and resurrection. Our good conscience thus testifies before God, before worldly people, before angels, before Satan, and before all created things that we are joined to Christ, that we have died and resurrected with Him, and that in Him we have received God's forgiveness of our sins, are justified by God, and have returned to God to eternally belong to Him.

Baptism is not a ceremony or ritual for becoming a church member; rather, it is a practical procedure, a definite step in faith. By such a step we enter into Christ and are joined to Him, obtain full salvation in Him, and have a silent testimony to His salvation from our good conscience.

THE MEANING OF THE WORD *BAPTISM*

1. "Baptized" (Mark 16:16).

Baptizo is the Greek word used here and in other places in the New Testament; it means "to dip in or under, to immerse, or to sink." This meaning is found in all the well-known Greek lexicons and is agreed upon by all the famous Bible scholars throughout the ages. Martin Luther, the leader of the Reformation, said that he hoped everyone who is baptized would have his whole body put into the water because that is the meaning of the word *baptism*. John Calvin was a great Bible expositor of the Reformation; he said that the meaning of the word *baptism* is to immerse and that this was the practice of the primitive church. Dean Stanley said that the practice of the first thirteen centuries was according to the New Testament and that the people went into the water according to the original meaning of the word *baptizo*.

THE PATTERN OF BAPTISM

1. "Having been baptized, Jesus went up immediately from the water" (Matt. 3:16).

God used a clear word *baptism* to tell us that baptism is to be put into water; He also used a pattern or example to show that baptism means to be put into water. People can explain the clear meaning of the word differently, but the pattern of the example eliminates differing human views. There are two patterns of baptism according to God's record in the Bible. The first is the baptism of the Lord Jesus. After our Lord was baptized, He went up from the water. This means that He first had to go into water. Going into water and coming up from water is the clear pattern established by our Lord Jesus. Should not all those who wish to follow in the footsteps of the Lord follow His pattern? If we want to be like the Lord and "fulfill all righteousness" before God (v. 15), how could we not follow His pattern or example by being baptized in a different way?

2. "They both went down into the water, Philip and the eunuch, and he baptized him. And when they came up out of the water" (Acts 8:38-39).

God not only provided the example of the baptism of the Lord Jesus in the Gospels; He also showed that the apostles followed the footsteps of the Lord in the book of Acts. Philip baptized the Ethiopian eunuch by going down into water and coming up out of water. By this we know how the early disciples baptized people. The record that they both went down into water and came up out of water is clear and accurate; how could people in later centuries have so much dissension and so many questions concerning the way to baptize people? Should we not go back to the beginning and follow these examples?

THE TYPE OF BAPTISM

1. "Entering into which [the ark], a few, that is, eight souls, were brought safely through by water. Which water, as the antitype, also now saves you, that is, baptism...through the resurrection of Jesus Christ" (1 Pet. 3:20-21).

In the Bible we have not only the pattern of baptism but also the type of baptism. In the Old Testament God used two events to paint a clear picture of the baptism which was to come in the New Testament; these two events prefigure baptism. The first event involved Noah's household passing through the flood in the ark. Through Peter the Holy Spirit said that this typifies baptism. This type not only clearly explains baptism, but it also shows the effect of baptism. The eight people of Noah's household who were in the ark were covered with water, showing that we should be covered with water in our baptism in Christ. The flood caused the people in the ark to be separated from the old world in which they had lived, freeing them from their corrupt generation. This shows that the water of baptism causes us, who are in Christ, to be separated from the world in which we live, freeing us from this crooked and perverted generation. Thus, just as they were saved by water and freed from their corrupted generation, we also are saved through the water of baptism and are freed from our crooked and perverted generation. On the one hand, they entered into the ark by faith and were saved by the ark from the flood waters of God's judgment; on the other hand, in the ark they passed through the flood and were saved by the flood waters from that old world and were given entrance into a new world. In the same way, we enter into Christ by faith and are saved in Christ from the judgment of God's wrath; we also pass through baptism in Christ and are saved through the water of baptism from the old world and are given entrance into the new realm of resurrection. They were saved through the ark from God's judgment, and they were saved in the ark by means of the flood waters from the old world; in the same way, we are saved through Christ from God's judgment, and we are saved in Christ by means of the water of baptism from the world to which we originally belonged. Just as the waters of the flood caused them to be separated from the world to which they originally belonged, the water baptism separates us from our old world. The waters of the flood through which they passed in the ark gave them entrance into a new world; in the same way, the water of baptism through Christ's death and resurrection gives us entrance into a new realm. Thus, the relationship of the floodwaters to the eight people of Noah's household typifies how baptism causes us to be saved by water from the world and into the realm of resurrection.

2. "All our fathers were under the cloud, and all passed through the sea; and all were baptized unto Moses in the cloud and in the sea" (1 Cor. 10:1-2).

The second event in the Old Testament that God used to

typify baptism is the Israelites' crossing of the Red Sea. The apostle Paul said that when the Israelites crossed the Red Sea, they were baptized. They crossed the Red Sea in the cloud and in the sea, signifying that our baptism should be in the Holy Spirit and in water. In the negative aspect, the Israelites' crossing of the Red Sea freed them from Pharaoh and Egypt, and in its positive aspect, it brought them to Moses. This signifies that our baptism frees us from Satan and the world under his hand and also brings us to Christ. Pharaoh and his army pursued the Israelites into the waters but could not cross the Red Sea to continue their pursuit; moreover, when the Israelites crossed the Red Sea, they were freed from Egypt and could not return to it or its living. This signifies that Satan and his authority can pursue us into the water of baptism but cannot cross this water. When we are baptized, we are freed from the world and cannot return to the worldly living. The water of the Red Sea buried Pharaoh and his army for the children of Israel, and it also saved the Israelites from Egypt and caused them to follow Moses to serve God. In the same way, on our behalf baptism destroys Satan and his power, and baptism also saves us from the world and causes us to follow Christ to serve God. Although the Israelites were saved by faith when they put the blood of the lamb on their doorposts, causing God's wrath to pass over them, they still needed to cross the Red Sea so that the power of Pharaoh over them could be destroyed. Although they were spared from God's judgment by keeping the passover, they would not have been able to escape from their slavery to Pharaoh and Egypt if they had not crossed the Red Sea. This tells us that even after receiving by faith the redemption of the Lord's shed blood and even with the removal of God's wrath, we must still cross the water of baptism so that Satan's power over us can be destroyed. Although we have believed in the Lord and are no longer condemned by God, we must be baptized in order to escape our slavery to Satan and the world. Therefore, baptism frees us from Satan and the world just as crossing the Red Sea freed the Israelites from Pharaoh and Egypt. Just as Pharaoh and his army followed the Israelites into the waters of the Red Sea and were drowned, the power of Satan and the world follows us into the waters of baptism and are destroyed there. We should bring all the things of the world that control and bind us into the water of baptism, such as fame, entertainment, money, fashion, movies, tobacco, and alcohol, and bury them. After Pharaoh and his army were drowned in the Red Sea, the Israelites were able to follow Moses to serve God. Similarly, Satan and the things of the world are buried in the water of baptism, but we come up in resurrection together with Christ and follow Him to serve God. The Red Sea is a type of our being saved through water and escaping the world and its power to enter into a new realm.

THE ONES BEING BAPTIZED

1. "He who believes and is baptized" (Mark 16:16).

Who can be baptized? Who is qualified to be baptized? Only a person who believes is qualified. This is because the Lord said, "He who believes and is baptized." This is a principle that does not and cannot change. Those who have not believed are absolutely not qualified to be baptized; only those who believe can be baptized. This believing must be a receiving of the Lord from the heart and must be a believing into the Lord—a receiving of the Lord into our being, allowing Him to enter into us and be mingled with us, and an entering into the Lord to be joined with Him, as we saw in chapter 5. This is not a mere mental belief in doctrines or an act of the will to enter a religion. A person who merely believes a doctrine or enters a religion does not believe in the Lord and does not contact the Lord, receive the Lord, enter into the Lord, or have a direct relationship with the Lord; therefore, he does not have the true and proper faith spoken of in the Bible. Faith in the Bible means to receive the Lord from one's heart, to use one's spirit to contact the Lord Himself, to enter into the Lord, to be joined to Him, and to enter into a life relationship with Him; it is not merely understanding some doctrines. Many understand gospel doctrines and many have received these doctrines, but they have not touched the Lord in their spirit to receive Him, so they cannot be considered as having believed in the Lord; thus, they are not qualified to be baptized. In contrast, some do not understand many doctrines, but they have prayed to the Lord from their heart and spirit and have received the Lord as their Savior. They have truly believed and can be baptized.

An infant, who does not even know the difference between his right and left hand, does not have the capacity to believe and is not qualified to be baptized. According to the principle of "believes and is baptized," infant baptism is absolutely not allowed. It is very much against the Bible.

2. "When they believed...the gospel...and of the name of Jesus Christ, they were baptized" (Acts 8:12).

In Samaria the ones who were baptized first believed the gospel and the name of the Lord Jesus. They did not only believe the gospel but also the name of the Lord. The gospel says that the Lord died for our sins, was buried, and rose on the third day (1 Cor. 15:1-4); that they believed the gospel means they believed that the Lord died for them and was buried and rose again. The name of the Lord speaks of His person and represents the Lord Himself. That they believed in the name of the Lord means they believed in the Lord Himself and received the Lord Himself (John 1:12). Since they believed in this way, they could be baptized, and they were.

3. "What prevents me from being baptized? And Philip said, If you believe from all your heart, you will be saved. And he answered and said, I believe that Jesus Christ is the Son of God" (Acts 8:36-37).

The conversation between the evangelist Philip and the Ethiopian eunuch shows that if a person believes from all his heart, nothing should prevent him from being baptized. However, we must note that it says, "Believe from all your heart." It does not tell us to believe with the mind or with the brain but from all the heart. This means our entire heart must believe; we cannot believe half-heartedly or with doubts. We must believe from all our heart before being baptized.

This shows the object of our faith. What do we believe? We believe that Jesus Christ is the Son of God. A person must believe that Jesus Christ is the Son of God in order to receive life in His name (John 20:31). Therefore, one must believe this from all his heart before he can be baptized. As soon as he believes in this way, he can be baptized; he does not need to wait until he understands many doctrines or wait for anything else.

4. "They heard, believed and were baptized" (Acts 18:8).

This word refers to the early Corinthians. They believed and were baptized. They had to believe before being baptized, but once they believed they could be baptized. We cannot be anything less than a believer, and we need not be anything more.

Note: First Corinthians 15:29 speaks of being "baptized for the dead." This is not God's ordination but a practice that some of the Corinthian believers made up. In this verse the apostle Paul based an argument upon this practice with those among the Corinthians who did not believe in the resurrection but who were practicing being baptized for the dead. He pointed out that their beliefs and actions were contradictory since they did not believe in resurrection but were practicing being baptized for the dead. God calls for only believing, living people to be baptized; He never asks someone to be baptized for a believer who died without being baptized. The saved criminal on the cross is an example of a believer who died without being baptized; his case is an example and proof of this point.

THE ONE BAPTIZING

1. "Jesus Himself did not baptize, but rather His disciples" (John 4:2).

When the Lord was on earth gaining disciples, He did not baptize; rather, His disciples baptized. We must pay attention to the fact that it does not say that His apostles baptized. It says that His disciples baptized. Of course, among the disciples there were apostles, but they did not baptize in their office as apostles but in their position as disciples. This tells us that the Lord had disciples do the baptizing. The disciples, the believers, baptized others. Thus, any believer who is a disciple of the Lord can baptize. The teaching that only the clergy can baptize or that only those with an office in the church can baptize was started and ordained by the Roman

Catholic Church. This poison of heresy was also brought into the Reformation from the Roman Catholic Church; this is against the teachings of the Bible and against the Lord's will. According to the Lord's will, a believer does not need to hold an office in the church in order to baptize. Baptism is not based on one's office in the church; rather, any saved believer can baptize someone in his status as a believer. Of course, anyone baptizing another person should carefully consider all sides of the matter and seek the Lord's leading.

  2. "Go...baptizing them" (Matt. 28:19).

The Lord's command to preach the gospel to the nations and to baptize the nations was given to the disciples, not to the apostles. Although the eleven who received this command were apostles, they are not called "the eleven apostles"; instead, they are called "the eleven disciples" in verse 16. When the Lord gave this command, He did not consider them to be apostles but disciples. If the Lord had considered them to be apostles when He gave the command, only a small number of apostles would have gone out to preach the gospel to the nations, and not all the disciples would have participated in this matter. This is not the Lord's intention. He wants all the disciples who believe in Him to preach the gospel to others and to baptize them. Anyone who is His disciple should preach the gospel and baptize people. Preaching the gospel is the heavenly occupation of His disciples, and baptizing people is their duty. Preaching the gospel and baptizing are two sides of the Lord's commission to His disciples. Both aspects are the responsibility of His disciples, and both are their authorized right. Therefore, whoever preaches the gospel has the authority to baptize.

  3. "A...disciple...named Ananias" (Acts 9:10, see also vv. 17-18).

When the Lord chose Paul to be an apostle, He did not send an apostle to baptize him; He sent a disciple named Ananias. The Bible does not tell us that Ananias held any office in the church; it says only that he was a disciple. This also shows that as long as one is a disciple, he can baptize others; one who baptizes does not need to hold any office in the church. Furthermore, when Paul went to Damascus, the church there may not have been officially established, so the Lord sent a disciple named Ananias to baptize him. This tells us that in any place where there is a church, any of the saints can baptize people together with the whole church, but in a place without a church, any of the scattered disciples can baptize. Of course, this is speaking in principle; we must follow the Lord's leading for the details, just as Ananias did.

4. "They both went down into the water, Philip and the eunuch, and he baptized him" (Acts 8:38).

Philip was not an apostle but an evangelist (21:8), yet he not only preached the gospel to the Ethiopian eunuch but also baptized him. This clearly tells us that whoever has the authority to preach the gospel can also baptize. Moreover, Philip was on a road in a place without a church, so he baptized the man by himself. This also proves that in places where there are no churches, the believers can baptize those to whom they preach the gospel. Of course, this is in principle; we must also follow the leading of the Holy Spirit as Philip did.

5. "I thank God that I baptized none of you except Crispus and Gaius" (1 Cor. 1:14; see also Acts 18:8).

Although many believed and were baptized when Paul first preached the gospel in Corinth, Paul baptized only a few of them, such as Crispus and Gaius. The other disciples baptized the rest. Paul and the other disciples' practice shows that baptism does not need to be carried out by an apostle sent by the Lord or by any other person with a spiritual office. The apostles sent by the Lord or those with spiritual offices can baptize people, but in places where there are brothers, it is best to be like Paul and not baptize so many; rather, we should allow the brothers to baptize lest there be an improper result.

Some who serve the Lord baptize many people, but this is not appropriate or according to the pattern left by the apostles. Some, however, based upon 1 Corinthians 1:17, only preach the gospel and never baptize others; this is not right either. This does not follow the footsteps left by the apostle. Although the apostle said that he was not sent out to baptize but to announce the gospel, he did baptize some. He clearly wrote of this in the preceding verses. What he meant was that the goal of his being sent out was not to baptize people but to announce the gospel; he was not saying that he never baptized anyone. When it was necessary, he baptized people; however, in places where there were brothers, he did not baptize many. It is best if there are brothers to participate in the baptizing to prevent anything inappropriate from occurring, but if there are no brothers, one must do it oneself.

THE TIME OF BAPTISM

1. "Those then who received his word were baptized" (Acts 2:41).

When a person believes in the Lord, he should be baptized immediately without waiting. On the day of Pentecost three thousand people received Peter's word, believed in the Lord, and were baptized. It was not like today when people believe in the Lord and wait many days before being baptized. Waiting is not according to the Bible, and it quenches the work of the Holy Spirit. There is no passage in the Bible which says that a person waited a long time between believing in the Lord and being baptized. The Bible indicates that when people believed in the Lord, they were immediately baptized. The acts of believing and being baptized should be close together; they should not be separated by a long period of time. When a person is moved by the Holy Spirit to believe, he should immediately be baptized; this will enable the Holy Spirit to work more strongly and more thoroughly in him. If he is not baptized immediately after believing and continues to wait, his heart will become heavy, and the Holy Spirit will be hindered from doing a strong, thorough work in him. Many believe, but they are not living or strong because they did not take advantage of the time immediately after believing, when their hearts were on fire, to be baptized. When a blacksmith pounds on metal to make scissors, he must heat the metal to the right temperature, beat it just the right way, and immediately plunge it into cold water to make the cutting edge sharp. If the metal cools after it is heated and is not pounded properly when it is hot, the cutting edge will be very dull when it is plunged into cold water. Many brothers and sisters do not have a strong salvation because they were not plunged into the cold water of baptism when their faith was burning hot. When someone believes in the Lord, he will suffer loss if he is not baptized immediately.

We have seen in the preceding sections that baptism is a procedural step for people to receive the Lord's salvation, through which people are put into the Lord and His death, and through which they are buried and resurrected together with Him. In a normal situation, the beginning step in receiving the Lord's salvation is to believe, and the completing step is to be baptized. Today, however, things are totally differently. Some wait for people to become completely clear about matters related to salvation before baptizing them. A wedding ceremony is the final step in a marriage procedure, but the experience of some related to baptism can be likened to people living as a married couple and then having a wedding ceremony much later to represent their act of being married. It is no wonder that among us some say that baptism is only a representation of our death, burial, and resurrection together with the Lord. To be baptized is to be put into the Lord's death, burial, and resurrection; it does not represent our death, burial, and resurrection with the Lord. When a person believes and is immediately baptized, his baptism puts him into the Lord's death, burial, and resurrection. If he waits a long time after believing before being baptized, his baptism will become merely a representation of his death, burial, and resurrection together with the Lord.

2. "When they believed…they were baptized" (Acts 8:12).

The Samaritans who heard the gospel from Philip believed and were baptized immediately. This is always the pattern in the Bible.

3. "I believe that Jesus Christ is the Son of God. And he ordered the chariot to stand still, and they both went down into the water, Philip and the eunuch" (Acts 8:37-38).

The Ethiopian eunuch believed in the Lord as he was traveling on a road. Even though it was not convenient to be baptized, he was still baptized immediately after believing.

4. "He took them with him in that very hour of the night and washed their wounds. And he was baptized immediately, he and all his household" (Acts 16:33).

The Philippian jailer and his household believed in the Lord in the middle of the night and were immediately baptized in that very hour. If we were responsible for the arrangements, we would have many reasons for waiting to baptize them, including: (1) They were Gentiles who had never known God or heard His word. Since they had heard His word only once, how could they be baptized immediately? They should wait to be baptized until they understood more of the word. (2) When they heard the Lord's word and believed, it was the middle of the night. To be baptized in the middle of the night is extremely inconvenient, so they should at least wait for daylight. (3) Paul and Silas had been beaten with rods and were covered with wounds. How could it be convenient for them to baptize anyone? They should wait at least for their wounds to heal before baptizing anyone. We would consider any of these reasons to be sufficient to make us wait. However, they did not consider even one of them, and they did not wait. Even though Paul and Silas were covered with wounds from being beaten and it was the middle of the night, they did not hesitate to baptize the jailer and his household once they had heard the gospel and believed. Paul and Silas did not hold back from baptizing the people at that very hour because they were covered with wounds or because it was too late at night, and they did not ask the people to wait for baptism because they did not understand more doctrines. They knew that understanding more of the Lord's Word comes after baptism, not before. Their practice was according to the Lord's command to preach the gospel and to baptize the ones who believed, and then to teach them the Lord's Word (Matt. 28:19-20). The gospel causes people to receive spiritual life, baptism brings people into the reality of their spiritual birth, and Bible teaching enables people who have received a spiritual birth to obtain spiritual nourishment and education. Nourishment and education come after our spiritual birth, so it is something that we receive after baptism. Some, however, require people to understand many doctrines before they can be baptized. This is like trying to educate a person before he is born. It is no wonder that the practice of baptism does not bring people into the reality of their spiritual birth but is only a representation of spiritual birth after it has occurred. Instead of entering into the reality of our spiritual birth through baptism, many are born spiritually and then only later represent this reality through baptism. The way that baptism often is practiced today does not benefit a person's spiritual life in the way that an immediate baptism would. This causes many to suffer loss; it is improper and unnecessary.

We think that people must hear and understand much of God's Word in order to be saved; actually, people are saved when they have spiritual contact with the Lord in their spirit. The gospel that we preach should open the way for people to have a living touch with the Lord. As long as a person has a living contact with the Lord through our gospel preaching, he can be baptized immediately without the need to understand many doctrines.

5. "Why do you delay? Rise up and be baptized and wash away your sins, calling on His name" (Acts 22:16).

Ananias spoke these words to Saul, who had been enlightened by the Lord and had believed in Him on the road to Damascus. Saul had only believed in the Lord for three days without being baptized (9:9), but the Holy Spirit rebuked him for delaying. Today, if a person is baptized only three days after believing, we might rebuke him for being too quick. But should we follow the will of the Holy Spirit or follow our own opinion? The Holy Spirit considers it a delay for someone to wait for three days in order to be baptized. Since the Lord wants people to be baptized immediately after believing, there should not be even one moment's delay. Thus, we should recover the matter of baptism so that the water of baptism always comes after the gospel message. As soon as people receive the gospel, they should immediately go into the water to be baptized. This is according to the Lord's will and the pattern of the Bible, and it results in great spiritual benefit. However, it requires faith and the power of the Holy Spirit. It requires us to preach the gospel in power, and it requires us to baptize people in faith. If we lack these two things, we are only imitating the black and white letters of the Bible and do not have the spiritual reality.

THE PLACE OF BAPTISM

1. "As they were going along the road, they came upon some water, and the eunuch said, Look, water. What prevents me from being baptized?" (Acts 8:36).

The Ethiopian eunuch was baptized as soon as he and Philip came upon some water beside the road. This shows that baptism is not tied to any place; the only thing necessary is water. When I first believed in the Lord, a pastor told me that if we had to imitate the Lord Jesus by going down into the water to be baptized, then we should imitate Him by being baptized in the Jordan River. But this is not the only pattern in the Bible; any place with water is good for baptism.

2. "John also was baptizing in Aenon near Salim, because there was much water there; and people came and were baptized" (John 3:23).

John was baptizing in Aenon near Salim because there was much water there. This indicates several things, including: (1) There should be much water in a place for baptism. Any place that has enough water to submerge people is good for baptism. (2) When John baptized people, he must have put them into the water, so there was a need for a place with much water. If baptism is only a ritual sprinkling or a ritual dripping, he would have needed only a little water. It would not have mattered how much water was in a particular place. Any place would have been fine. In order to submerge people in water, however, he needed a place with much water.

THE CORRECTION OF BAPTISM

1. "He said, Into what then were you baptized? And they said, Into John's baptism. And Paul said, John baptized with a baptism of repentance, telling the people that they should believe into the One coming after him, that is, into Jesus. And when they heard this, they were baptized into the name of the Lord Jesus" (Acts 19:3-5).

This passage speaks of the disciples in Ephesus, who were baptized with John's baptism of repentance and did not know that John led people to believe in the Lord Jesus. They also did not know that once the Lord Jesus came to minister, John's baptism of repentance had ceased and that people should be baptized into the name of the Lord Jesus. When they learned this, they immediately corrected the problem and were baptized into the name of the Lord Jesus. Thus, according to the pattern recorded in the Bible, if a person is not baptized properly, his baptism can be corrected. In those days the baptism of repentance had ceased and was inadequate, so anyone baptized in that way needed a correction. Today there are rituals of sprinkling, dripping, infant baptism, baptism before one properly believes, and baptism before one has contacted the Lord in spirit. All of these are improper, and anyone baptized in such a way should correct it. When it is corrected, it should be carried out by faith in order to receive all the spiritual realities of baptism.

Chapter Eighteen

THE LAYING ON OF HANDS

I. A foundational doctrine.
II. The meaning of the laying on of hands:
    A. Joining.
    B. Fellowship.
III. The kinds of laying on of hands:
    A. The laying on of hands for acceptance:
        1. After baptism.
        2. For receiving into the Body of Christ.
        3. The relationship between the laying on of hands and baptism.
    B. The laying on of hands for receiving the Holy Spirit.
    C. The laying on of hands for the impartation of gifts.
    D. The laying on of hands for appointment.
    E. The laying on of hands for sending out.
    F. The laying on of hands for blessing.
    G. The laying on of hands for healing.
IV. Caution in the laying on of hands.

The laying on of hands is something people should receive after believing and being baptized.

A FOUNDATIONAL DOCTRINE

1. "The word of the beginning of Christ...a foundation of repentance from dead works and of faith in God, of the teaching of baptisms and of the laying on of hands, of the resurrection of the dead and of eternal judgment" (Heb. 6:1-2).

The Holy Spirit speaks here of six foundational teachings: repentance, faith, baptisms, the laying on of hands, resurrection, and judgment. These are divided into three pairs: first, repentance and faith; second, baptisms and the laying on of hands; and third, resurrection and judgment. The first teaching in each pair emphasizes escape on the negative side, and the second teaching emphasizes entrance on the positive side. Repentance is from dead works, and faith is in God. Baptisms enable us to escape from negative things, and the laying on of hands enables us to enter into a proper position and to obtain positive things. Resurrection enables us to be delivered from death and the realm of death, and judgment enables us to enter into a new world. Since the laying on of hands is one of the foundational teachings and is the positive aspect of the second pair of teachings, we should pay attention to it. Many stress repentance, faith, baptisms, resurrection, and judgment but neglect the laying on of hands. The Holy Spirit, however, lists the laying on of hands among these foundational teachings and considers it to be of equal importance with the others.

THE MEANING OF THE LAYING ON OF HANDS

Many in today's Christianity see the laying on of hands as a ritual and a rite of ordination. This view is not according to the Bible. In the Bible there are two important meanings related to the laying on of hands, which show that it exceeds the status of a rite or ritual.

Joining

1. "He shall lay his hand on the head of the sin offering" (Lev. 4:29, see also vv. 2-4; 8:14).

In the Old Testament, when a person came before God to present a sin offering, he laid his hand on the head of the sacrificial animal to signify that he was joined with the offering, making himself one with the sacrifice. Without being one with the sacrifice, the animal could not take his place and cause his sins to be expiated. This is because vicarious redemption is based on the joining of the one redeemed and the substitute. If we are not joined to the Lord, we cannot have Him as our Substitute. The redeemed one must be joined to the Substitute, or Redeemer, in order to be redeemed and for the redemption to be effective. Without this joining, there is no substitution. If a sinner wanted to put his sins onto a sacrifice in order for them to be expiated, he had to join himself to the sacrifice. Consequently, the person offering a sin offering had to place his hand on the head of the sacrifice in order to be joined to the sacrifice. This shows that joining is the first meaning of the laying on of hands.

2. "He shall lay his hand on the head of the burnt offering" (Lev. 1:4; see also 8:18).

In the Old Testament in order to signify the joining of himself to the sacrifice, a person not only had to lay his hand on the head of the sin offering, but he also had to lay his hand on the head of the burnt offering. The one presenting a burnt offering had to be joined to the animal being sacrificed for him in order to be acceptable to God. Thus, he had to lay his hand upon the head of the sacrifice in order to be joined to the sacrifice. Therefore, in the Bible joining is the first meaning of the laying on of hands.

Fellowship

1. "Lay your hand upon him...put some of your honor upon him" (Num. 27:18-20).

The second meaning of the laying on of hands is fellowship. When there is the laying on of hands, there is a spontaneous fellowship. When we lay our hand on a head, there is fellowship, that is, the giving of something that we have to others. Fellowship is similar to a battery that gives some of its electricity to a loudspeaker through its connection to it. In this passage God told Moses to lay his hand on the head of Joshua;

this was for Moses to have fellowship with Joshua so that Moses could put some of his honor on Joshua. In the laying on of hands, the one laying on his hands and the person having hands laid upon him have fellowship, and the one laying on his hands passes some of his blessing to the person having hands laid upon him.

2. **"The gift of God, which is in you through the laying on of my hands"** (2 Tim. 1:6; see also 1 Tim. 4:14).

Paul had the gift of God, and when he laid his hands on Timothy, he had fellowship with him. He, thereby, gave Timothy some of his gift in that fellowship.

In the Bible the meaning of the laying on of hands is joining and fellowship. In 2 Kings 13:14-17 both can be found. Elisha laid his hands on the king of Israel and was joined to the king and had fellowship with the king. On the one hand, he was joined to the king of Israel to fight the enemies of Israel; on the other hand, he passed his overcoming power to the king of Israel through fellowship.

THE KINDS OF LAYING ON OF HANDS

According to the Bible, there are at least seven kinds of laying on of hands.

The Laying On of Hands for Acceptance

The first kind of laying on of hands is the laying on of hands for acceptance.

After Baptism

1. **"Baptisms and of the laying on of hands"** (Heb. 6:2).

According to the order recorded in verse 2, the laying on of hands for acceptance should come after baptism. This indicates that after a person is baptized, we should lay hands on him to receive him.

2. **"They were baptized into the name of the Lord Jesus. And when Paul laid his hands on them"** (Acts 19:5-6; see also 8:16-17).

The early believers in Ephesus were first baptized, and then the apostle laid his hands on them. It was the same with

the believers in Samaria. The laying on of hands for acceptance should always take place after baptism. Because there
was no one to baptize him when he believed, Saul of Tarsus
first received the laying on of hands and then was baptized
(9:17-18). In order to prove he had been sent by the Lord,
Ananias had to first lay his hands on Saul so that his eyes
could be opened and so that he could receive the filling of the
Holy Spirit. Ananias first laid his hands on Saul, and then he
had Saul make up his baptism.

For Receiving into the Body of Christ

**1. "He [the Holy Spirit] had not yet fallen upon any
of them, but they had only been baptized into the name
of the Lord Jesus. Then they laid their hands on them,
and they received the Holy Spirit"** (Acts 8:16-17).

The laying on of hands is also for receiving one who has
been baptized into Christ in order to bring him into the church,
the Body of Christ. The early Samaritan believers were baptized into Christ, but they had not received the outpouring
of the Holy Spirit, because the apostles had not laid hands
upon them. Later, when the apostles laid hands on them,
it seems as if they merely received the Holy Spirit, but there
is a deeper implication as well. The laying on of hands by the
apostles caused them to receive the Holy Spirit because the
anointing of the Holy Spirit was poured out upon the Head,
Christ, and on the day of Pentecost it flowed from the Head
to the Body, the church. Since the apostles are representatives
of the Body, when they laid their hands on people, they represented the Body and received them into the Body. Thus, the
anointing on the Body, which is the Holy Spirit, flows to the
ones brought in through the laying on of hands. Therefore,
hands are laid on believers after baptism to receive them
into the Body of Christ and to allow them to participate in the
Holy Spirit, which the Body received from the Head, Christ.

**2. "When Paul laid his hands on them, the Holy
Spirit came upon them"** (Acts 19:6).

Paul laid his hands on the Ephesian believers, causing
them to receive the Holy Spirit; this is the same thing that
Peter and John did for the Samaritan believers. Paul was a

representative of the Body of Christ, and through the laying on of hands, he received those who were baptized into Christ into the Body, causing the anointing, the Holy Spirit (Psa. 133:2), who flows from the Head to the Body, to flow through him to those on whom he laid his hands.

Thus, the laying on of hands is for receiving people into the Body of Christ; therefore, those who lay hands on others must be able to represent the Body of Christ, the church. When they lay hands on people, they represent the church, and their laying on of hands is the church's laying on of hands in order to receive them into the church and to cause them to participate in the things of Christ and the church.

The Relationship between
the Laying On of Hands and Baptism

1. "Baptisms and of the laying on of hands" (Heb. 6:2).

We mentioned before that baptism and the laying on of hands have been connected as a pair by the Holy Spirit. This shows that the laying on of hands is related to baptism. The laying on of hands should be based on baptism, and baptism should bring in the laying on of hands. In its negative application, baptism causes people to escape from the self and the world, and in its positive application, it causes them to enter into Christ. The laying on of hands causes those who have escaped the self and the world and have been put into Christ through baptism to enter into the Body of Christ. Thus, baptism stresses individual salvation, and the laying on of hands stresses the building up of the Body of Christ. If we have only baptism without the laying on of hands, we will pay attention only to individual salvation but neglect the Body of Christ. God, however, saves individuals for the purpose of building up the Body of Christ. He led Philip to baptize the Samaritan believers into Christ, and then He sent Peter and John, who represented the Body of Christ, to lay hands on them and to receive them into the Body of Christ (Acts 8:12-17). He saves people in order to make them the Body of Christ. This is similar to a person who buys many stones for the purpose of building them into a house; if he does not build the house, his purchase has no meaning. He must build the stones into a house in order for them to be useful. Therefore, we should not only lead people to believe and be baptized into Christ but also lay hands on them to receive them into the Body of Christ. We want many not only to be saved but also to be brought into the Body of Christ so that everyone can be coordinated together, supply one another, and function corporately. We must pay attention to getting many people saved, and we must also pay attention to building up the Body of Christ. We must stress personal salvation, and we must also stress the service of the Body. Moreover, we must lead people to salvation with the goal of building up the Body of Christ. We are individually saved for the service of the Body. Thus, we should pay equal attention to baptism and to the laying on of hands; we must see that baptism is for the laying on of hands and that the laying on of hands completes baptism.

The Laying On of Hands
for Receiving the Holy Spirit

The second kind of laying on of hands is for receiving the Holy Spirit. This kind of laying on of hands is similar to the laying on of hands for acceptance, which also involves receiving the Holy Spirit. These two kinds of laying on of hands are actually one, and the results of their two functions are connected. The function of receiving people into the Body of Christ is connected to the function of receiving the Holy Spirit because when a person is received into the Body of Christ, he spontaneously receives the Holy Spirit, who is on the Body. Similarly, when a person receives the Holy Spirit, he becomes a part of the Body (1 Cor. 12:13).

1. "He had not yet fallen upon any of them...Then they laid their hands on them, and they received the Holy Spirit" (Acts 8:16-17).

The Samaritan believers believed and were baptized into Christ, but the Holy Spirit did not fall upon any of them until Peter and John came and laid their hands upon them. Therefore, the apostles' laying on of hands caused them to receive the Holy Spirit.

2. "Did you receive the Holy Spirit when you believed?...And when Paul laid his hands on them, the Holy Spirit came upon them" (Acts 19:1-6).

The Ephesian believers, like the Samaritans, did not receive the Holy Spirit until the apostle laid his hands upon them. Paul laid his hands on them, causing them to receive the Holy Spirit.

3. "Ananias...laying his hands on him...said, Saul, brother, the Lord has sent me...so that you may...be filled with the Holy Spirit" (Acts 9:17).

The Lord sent Ananias to lay his hands on Saul so that Saul could be filled with the Holy Spirit, that is, so that he could receive the Holy Spirit.

The preceding three passages speak of representatives of the Body of Christ laying their hands on new believers so that the anointing on the Body of Christ could flow to them and so that they could receive the Holy Spirit who is on the Body of Christ. These representatives of the Body of Christ were living in the Body and had the Holy Spirit, who is on the Body, on themselves. Therefore, when they laid their hands on the new believers, they not only represented the Body to receive the new ones, but they also communicated the Holy Spirit who was upon them to the new believers. The Holy Spirit upon them was like electricity that could pass to those whom they laid their hands on, causing them to receive the Holy Spirit and to participate in the Body of Christ.

The Laying On of Hands
for the Impartation of Gifts

The third kind of laying on of hands is for the impartation of gifts by which a person with a gift imparts his gift to another through the laying on of hands.

1. "The gift of God, which is in you through the laying on of my hands" (2 Tim. 1:6).

Paul, through the laying on of his hands, imparted his gift into Timothy. The gift in Paul was transmitted to Timothy through the laying on of hands.

2. "The gift which is in you...by means of prophecy

with the laying on of the hands of the presbytery"
(1 Tim. 4:14).

This must refer to the matter in 2 Timothy 1:6. Paul laid
his hands on Timothy with the elders in the church in order
for Timothy to obtain a gift. Paul was an apostle, and an
apostle represents the universal church. The elders of the
church represent the local church. The apostle and the elders
together represent the entire church, the Body of Christ.
Christ gave all His gifts to the Body, the church (cf. Eph. 4;
Rom. 12; 1 Cor. 12). The apostle and the elders joined together
to lay hands on Timothy and were the representatives of the
Body so that the gifts given by the Head to the Body could be
dispensed to one of the members.

In ancient times Moses dispensed his glory and honor to
Joshua through the laying on of his hand (Num. 27:18-20),
and the angel Gabriel gave Daniel insight with understanding through the laying on of hands (Dan. 9:21-22, Chinese
Union Version). In principle, these instances of the laying on
of hands were for the impartation of gifts.

The Laying On of Hands for Appointment

The fourth kind of laying on of hands is to appoint someone to do something.

**1. "Appoint over this need...Whom they set before
the apostles; and when they had prayed, they laid their
hands on them"** (Acts 6:3, 6).

In the early church in Jerusalem, the apostles appointed
seven brothers in the church to be responsible for the daily
dispensing of food; after praying for them, they laid their
hands on them. The apostles' laying on of hands was related
to their appointment for the daily dispensing of food. This
kind of laying on of hands can be called the laying on of hands
for appointment. However, we must never think that the
laying on of hands for appointment is some kind of ordination
ritual. The purpose of this kind of laying on of hands is for
fellowship and identification. When the early apostles laid
their hands on the seven brothers, they were having fellowship with them, causing them to receive the grace needed for
the daily dispensing of food. Simultaneously, they were joined

to them, participating in their service and bearing the responsibility for this ministry with them in spirit.

The Laying On of Hands for Sending Out

The fifth kind of laying on of hands is the laying on of hands to send some out for the work, so it is the laying on of hands for sending out. The laying on of hands for appointment causes the recipients to receive a service within a church; the laying on of hands for sending out causes the recipient to go out into the work.

1. **"When they had fasted and prayed and laid their hands on them, they sent them away"** (Acts 13:3).

In the early church in Antioch, there were five prophets and teachers, three of whom laid hands on the other two in order to send them out to do the work to which God had called them. This kind of laying on of hands for sending out also has the purpose of joining and fellowship. The three who laid their hands on the two indicated that they were one with the two as they went out to do the work for God. They were joined to the two and had fellowship with them. When the two went out, the three also went with them. Although the three could not go out with them physically, they went with them in spirit through the laying on of hands. We must firmly grasp this principle, and we should imitate this practice. Every time some brothers receive a calling from God or are sent out for the work, we should be joined to them and have fellowship with them; their going should be the entire church's going. The entire church, through its representatives, lays its hands on those going out in order to be joined to them and to go out with them. This kind of laying on of hands in the church is not an empty ritual; rather, it is a spiritual reality that causes the recipients of the laying on of hands to be supplied by the whole church in their service to God so that they would not be alone or act individualistically. Under the proper conditions, this kind of laying on of hands causes the recipients to receive the Lord's blessing and the power of the Holy Spirit.

The preceding five kinds of laying on of hands are all related to the Body of Christ. Although their outward function is somewhat different, their inward meaning is the same.

Whether it be the laying on of hands for acceptance, for receiving of the Holy Spirit, for the impartation of spiritual gifts, for appointment, or for sending out, the inward meaning is always joining and fellowship.

The Laying On of Hands for Blessing

The sixth kind of laying on of hands is for blessing, which causes people to be blessed through the laying on of hands.

1. "Taking them into His arms, He fervently blessed them, laying His hands on them" (Mark 10:16; see also Gen. 48:14-16).

When the Lord Jesus was on earth, He laid His hands on the little children and blessed them. In the Old Testament Jacob laid his hands on his grandchildren and blessed them. This also implies fellowship.

The Laying On of Hands for Healing

There is yet another kind of laying on of hands, which causes people to be healed, so it is the laying on of hands for healing.

1. "He laid His hands on each one of them and healed them" (Luke 4:40).

When the Lord Jesus was on earth, He laid His hands on many sick people to heal them.

2. "They will lay hands on the sick, and they will be well" (Mark 16:18).

After the Lord Jesus ascended into the heavens, the disciples also laid their hands on people to heal them.

3. "Paul went in to him, and having prayed and laid his hands on him, healed him" (Acts 28:8).

Paul laid his hands on people to heal them. This kind of laying on of hands for healing also has the meaning of fellowship because it gives the sick one the gift of healing through fellowship with the one laying on his hands; this heals the sick one.

CAUTION IN THE LAYING ON OF HANDS

1. "Lay hands quickly on no man, nor participate in others' sins; keep yourself pure" (1 Tim. 5:22).

Since the laying on of hands joins people in fellowship, if someone is sinful and unclean, the person laying on his hands would participate in the other's sinfulness and uncleanness. Therefore, when we lay hands on people, we must be cautious and not act too quickly lest we participate in the sins of others. For the sake of keeping ourselves pure, we must discern before we lay hands on him whether the person whom we intend to lay our hands on has rejected sin and dealt clearly with evil before God and man. If he has not, we should not lay our hands on him.

CHAPTER NINETEEN

HEAD COVERING

I. The teaching of head covering:
   A. Handed down by the apostle Paul.
   B. To the saints in every place.
II. The meaning of head covering:
   A. A sign of submission to authority.
III. The basis for head covering:
   A. Based on the fact that God is the Head.
   B. Based on God's arrangement for men and women.
   C. Based on God's order in creation.
   D. Based on the problem with the angels.
   E. Based on human nature.
IV. The persons covering their heads:
   A. Women praying or prophesying.
V. The time of head covering:
   A. The time of prayer or prophesying.
VI. The object which covers the head:
   A. Long hair not replacing an object which covers the head.
   B. Long hair being God's arrangement and head covering being man's acceptance.
VII. The type of head covering:
   A. Rebekah.
   B. The high priest and the priests.
VIII. The relationship between head covering and the breaking of bread:
   A. Head covering being related to the Head and the breaking of bread being related to the Body.
   B. Head covering being a matter of authority and the breaking of bread being a matter of life.

The topic of head covering is ignored by many, but others pay much attention to it. Consequently, it is a subject of debate. Therefore, we must spend some time to see what God's Word says about this topic.

THE TEACHING OF HEAD COVERING

Handed Down by the Apostle Paul

1. "The things that I [the apostle Paul] have handed down...to you" (1 Cor. 11:2).

The teaching of head covering belongs to the New Testament and is taught by the apostle Paul. Since the New Testament emphasizes spiritual realities instead of outward rituals, we should not consider this teaching to be an outward ritual or something related to human thought. The apostle Paul preached according to the Lord's revelation, not man's thought (Gal. 1:11-12).

Some say that covering the head was an ordinance of the Jews. When the apostle Paul received a revelation from God, he set aside Judaism and all its ordinances; he absolutely did not preach Jewish ordinances to the church or ask the church to observe them. He did not even require the churches to keep the ordinance of circumcision which was established by God in the Old Testament (5:11). Therefore, why would he preach any other Jewish ordinance? On the contrary, he does not want us to keep any human ordinance (Col. 2:20-23). Moreover, the way the high priest and the other priests approached God was absolutely the opposite of what Paul teaches concerning head covering. Paul says that when a man prays or prophesies, he should not cover his head (1 Cor. 11:4), but the Jewish high priest and the other priests (all of whom were men) had to cover their heads when they approached God. The high priest had to wear a turban and crown on his head, and the other priests had to wear high hats (Lev. 8:7-9, 13). Thus, the teaching of head covering handed down by Paul is absolutely not related to Jewish ordinances.

Others say that head covering was a custom in Corinth at that time. However, we have the assurance that Paul would not use Gentile customs as part of his preaching or connect a

Gentile custom with the spiritual teachings concerning God and Christ that the church would then have to keep. He uses half a chapter of the Bible to speak of head covering, saying that this matter is related to God and Christ and that it influences the angels. When speaking of such a crucial matter, how could he use a Gentile custom as his background and base? Paul's teaching of head covering absolutely is not related to a Gentile custom.

To the Saints in Every Place

1. "To...all those who call upon the name of our Lord Jesus Christ in every place" (1 Cor. 1:2).

Some say that Paul's teaching concerning head covering was only for the church in Corinth because there was some confusion among them. This, however, is not accurate because the Epistle to the Corinthians, which contains the teaching concerning head covering, was written not only to the Corinthians, but to "all those who call upon the name of our Lord Jesus Christ in every place." Thus, the apostle's teaching concerning head covering was not only for the saints in Corinth; it was for all those who believe in the Lord in every place.

2. "If anyone seems to be contentious, we do not have such a custom of being so, neither the churches of God" (1 Cor. 11:16).

According to the apostle, the early churches of God did not have contentions concerning the teaching of head covering. This proves that the teaching was for all the churches, not only for the church in Corinth. Since this teaching was for all the churches and because the early apostles and churches accepted it without contention, should we not also receive it without contention?

THE MEANING OF HEAD COVERING

A Sign of Submission to Authority

1. "A sign of submission to authority on her head" (1 Cor. 11:10).

A more direct translation of this phrase is "to have authority on her head." The head signifies authority. According to

God's ordination, a woman, even though she has her own head, should not be the head but should submit to authority. Thus, she should cover her head as a confession and declaration that even though she has her own head, she is not the head and does not act as head. Head covering declares that she is under authority and confesses and receives another as her head, allowing him to be the head. Simply speaking, when the woman covers her head, it is a sign that she submits to authority.

THE BASIS FOR HEAD COVERING

Based on the Fact That God Is the Head

1. "I want you to know that Christ is the head of every man, and the man is the head of the woman, and God is the head of Christ. Every man praying or prophesying with his head covered disgraces his head. But every woman praying or prophesying with her head uncovered disgraces her head" (1 Cor. 11:3-5).

Some would say that the apostle taught head covering because it was an ordinance or custom of his time. They think the apostle's teaching of head covering was based upon ancient ordinances and customs. This kind of thinking comes from human speculation; it is not according to scriptural revelation. In 1 Corinthians 11 the apostle clearly says that he taught head covering based on the fact that God is the head. He based his teaching on the order of the universe in which God is the head, and he wanted us to know that this was the basis for his teaching of head covering.

In the universe created by God, there is a head, an authority, and an order. The head is God Himself. God is the head of the universe, the authority of the universe, and He causes the universe to be orderly. The first level of this order is that God is the head of Christ. Even though Christ is equal with God (Phil. 2:6), He was willing to submit to God's authority and allow God to be the head for the sake of expressing God as the head with authority and glory and so that God's orderly arrangement in the universe would be beautifully manifested. On this level, the Lord always submits to God and respects

God as the head. During His life on earth, He did nothing from Himself as the Lord; rather, He allowed God to be head. He never once assumed the headship or failed to manifest God as His head. He was the Lord and He had authority, yet He always allowed God to be His head and to cover His head in every matter. Oh, during His life on earth, there was such an expression with Him of God's authority and glory in the headship! His submission beautifully manifested God's orderly arrangement in the universe. He was not like this only while on earth, but even now He is like this in the heavens, and He will be like this for eternity. He submits to God eternally so that God may be all in all (1 Cor. 15:28).

God is the head of Christ, and Christ is the head of every man. This is the second level of God's orderly arrangement of the universe. On the one hand, God is the head of Christ, and on the other hand, He established Christ as the head of every one of us. On the one hand, Christ takes God as His head, but on the other hand, He is the head of every one of us. Just as God wants to receive Christ's submission, He also wants Christ to receive our submission. We must submit to Christ in the same way that He submits to God. Just as Christ allows God to be the head in all things and to cover His head, we also must allow Christ to be the head in all things and to cover our heads. As Christ is to God, so we must be to Him. He expresses God's authority and glory in God's headship over Him, and we must express Christ's authority and glory in His headship over us. He manifests the beauty of God's orderly arrangement in the universe, and we should do likewise. Oh, what can manifest God's authority and glorify God better than our submission to Him! What can manifest the beauty of God's arrangement of the universe better than our submission to the Lord! What can satisfy God's heart more than this submission! When we submit to the Lord and allow Him to be Head in all things, God is glorified greatly in us, and God's heart is satisfied in us. Since God's heart's desire for us is that Christ would be glorified in us just as He is glorified in Christ, He works in us to cause us to submit to Christ just as Christ submits to Him. All of God's work in us is to cause us to be unto the obedience of Christ (2 Cor. 10:5) and to confess and allow Christ to be the head of every man.

God not only wants Christ to be our head; He also wants the man to be the head of the woman. Thus, in His ordained arrangement, there is another level in which the man is the head of the woman. God established Christ as the head of every person, and He wants every person to take Christ as the head. However, He also established the man as the head of the woman, and He wants the woman to take the man as her head and to obey the man. Before Christ, none of us is male or female, so we should all take Him as our head; however, before humans, we are male and female, so we should be according to God's arrangement, and the man should be the head of the woman. The woman should take the man as her head and obey the man.

We should not bring the thought of the equality of men and women into this matter. This is not a question of whether men and women are equal; rather, it is a question of the function of men and women before God. God has an arrangement in which He wants two groups, men and women, to portray how He and Christ are the head and how humans should obey. God wants men to take the role of Himself and Christ, and He wants women to take the role of the submitting humans; therefore, when both groups, men and women, portray this, we can say that we have become a spectacle (a show) to the world, both to angels and to men (1 Cor. 4:9). Our spectacle displays the reality in the universe that there is a head and that there are those who obey. In this show, men and women are only the roles that we play; men portray how God and Christ are the head, and women portray how humans should obey. Since the functions in the roles that we play are different, it is not a matter of men and women being equal. Before the Lord men and women are both redeemed creatures without the slightest difference, but when we come before people, we must differentiate between men and women to portray the role of the head and the role of those who submit. This is similar to actors who are ordinary people off the stage but who play very particular characters in different roles on stage. When they act on the stage, there is a sense that they are different in function, but there is no thought of inequality. We should be like this. We have to see that the difference between men and women is a difference only in function; there is no thought of inequality. Simply because our eyes are below the eyebrows and there is a difference in function between them, are they unequal? The brothers have been given the role of the head to portray. Other than acknowledging that this is a great honor, is there any basis for brothers to be proud or to set themselves over others? Although the sisters have been given the role of the submitting ones to portray, does this mean that sisters are in some way despicable and should not also see the honor in their role? If I have been given a role that helps to demonstrate and manifest the Lord's authority and glory, even if the role is a lowly one, should I not feel that this is the greatest honor? If I take a man as my head and obey him and by so doing cause others to realize that God and Christ are the head whom they should obey, I would be so happy and feel that this is such an honor. Oh, may God show the sisters that their submission can cause people to sense the authority and glory of God and Christ! In the universe the sisters have this function with respect to God and Christ; it is an extremely glorious matter. They can demonstrate the beauty of God's orderly arrangement in the universe through their submission. This is a very sweet matter.

If the universe did not have a head, everything would be a mess. Since the universe has a head, God, there is order in the universe. God wants men and women to acknowledge this order by having men not cover their head and by having women cover theirs. If men were to cover their heads, it would be a shame to their head; that is, it would be a shame to Christ because Christ is the head of each one. Moreover, to shame Christ is to shame God, because God is the head of Christ. If a woman does not cover her head, it is a shame to her head and a direct shame to the man; it is also an indirect shame to Christ and to God because the man is the head of the woman, and Christ represents God as the head of each one of us. Thus, a man should not cover his head, and a woman should cover hers as a practical action to represent our acknowledgment of God as the authority in the universe—He is head in the universe. When the apostle Paul speaks about the teaching of head covering, he uses the headship of God as the first basis. Humans consider this a light matter, but God considers it a matter of great importance.

Based on God's Arrangement for Men and Women

1. **"A man ought not to have his head covered, since he is God's image and glory; but the woman is the glory of the man"** (1 Cor. 11:7).

Regardless of whether we are male or female, we are all out from God. He wants those who are male and those who are female to have distinctive functions. Therefore, He has a different arrangement for males and females. Under His arrangement He wants men to be His image and glory, and He wants women to be the glory of the man. For the sake of manifesting this arrangement, He uses the matter of head covering. Since the manifestation of men and women is different, He differentiates between men and women in the matter of head covering. Man is the image and glory of God; he is God's representative. Consequently, he should not cover his head as a sign that he represents God as the head. The woman is the glory of the man; she is the representation of humanity. Consequently, she should cover her head as a sign that she represents human submission. The different representative functions of men and women do not come from human will or human teachings but from God's will and God's arrangement. This divine arrangement is the second basis for the apostle's teaching concerning head covering.

Based on God's Order in Creation

1. **"Man is not out of woman, but woman out of man; for also man was not created for the sake of the woman, but woman for the sake of the man. Therefore the woman ought to have a sign of submission to authority on her head for the sake of the angels...For just as the woman is out from the man, so also is the man through the woman"** (1 Cor. 11:8-10, 12).

The arrangement of God's will for men and women is different. In the order of God's creation, there is a difference between men and women. First, He created the man, and then He created the woman. Furthermore, the woman is out of the man and for the man; the man is not out of the woman or for the woman. Although men are born through women, they are only "through" the woman, not "out from" the woman as the woman is "out from" the man. God's creation of men and women is different, and God's purpose for men and women is also different. According to His creation, the woman is out from the man, but the man is not out from the woman; according to His purpose, the woman is for the man, but the man is not for the woman. "Therefore the woman ought to have a sign of submission to authority on her head" (v. 10). She should have something covering her head.

God's creation and purpose for men and women are completely different. Man is man and woman is woman, just as bronze is bronze and iron is iron. No matter how much people argue, they cannot make women into men, and no matter how the fashion changes, they cannot make men into women. Since God's creation and purpose for men and women are different, the nature and function of men and women are also different. No one can deny this or overthrow this fact. This fact is the third basis for the apostle's teaching on head covering.

Based on the Problem with the Angels

1. "The woman ought to have a sign of submission to authority on her head for the sake of the angels" (1 Cor. 11:10).

The apostle does not want a woman to cover her head because of an ancient custom, as some suggest; rather, it is for the sake of the angels, as revealed by the Holy Spirit through the apostle. If he wanted women to cover their head because of an ancient custom, his teaching would not be worth considering, nor would it be related to people today. It could change with the age and be annulled by differing customs. Instead, he speaks of women covering their heads for the sake of the angels. This means we should be very impressed with this matter. Since this teaching is for the sake of angels, it cannot change with the age or customs. It cannot go out of date or be inappropriate for today. "For the sake of the angels" crosses time and customs. Regardless of the age or the custom, women should cover their heads for the sake of the angels.

What is the meaning of "for the sake of the angels"? This is deep and broad, and it requires many passages of the Bible for its interpretation. Briefly stated, this is the situation: When God first created the heavens and the earth, He appointed an archangel, a cherub, to govern the universe. This archangel lifted himself up because of his pride, and he rebelled against God, becoming Satan. When he rebelled, other angels followed him in his rebellion. All of this occurred before the creation of man. From that point forward, Satan and the rebellious angels who followed him did not submit to God's authority, and they tried to overthrow God's authoritative position. Therefore, God created man with the desire that man would submit to His authority and express His glory. Realizing this, Satan came to tempt man and to cause man to rebel against God and to follow him. He captured man. Through the Lord Jesus, however, God rescued us from Satan's hand and made us the church. As people saved by God, the church should confess God's authority and allow God to be the head. God wants us to have head covering to manifest this matter. We should practice head covering for the sake of the angels, showing them that created and redeemed men submit to God's authority, confess God as the head, and allow God to be the head, even though they do not. We confess that God is the head, allow Him to be the head, and submit to His authority. This is the fourth basis for the apostle's teaching of head covering.

Our practice of head covering glorifies God and, at the same time, shames Satan and the angels who followed him. Through head covering we confess that God is the head, and we shame them. This is one reason that God desires sisters to cover their heads. This is also the very reason that Satan causes people in the church to despise, neglect, and even oppose the matter of head covering. He knows that if the sisters cover their heads, it will be a shame to him.

Therefore, we should not consider head covering to be a small matter, and the sisters should not think that it does not matter whether or not they cover their heads, that is, whether or not they have a sign of submission to authority on their heads. If the citizens of a country fly their flag while their country is under enemy invasion, they are maintaining their country's authority and defying the enemy's invasion. Therefore, their flying of the flag is not a small thing. Head covering is the same because it displays a symbol of submission to God's authority in a place that has been taken over by God's enemy; it demonstrates our confession of God's authority and rejects Satan's illegal occupation. If we see the significance of this aspect of head covering, we will not have any dissension nor will we continue to allow Satan to have this as a basis for his continuing rebellion against God. We must allow God to thoroughly clean out Satan's rebellious thoughts and life from within us so that our thoughts and ideas would be completely recovered from his deceit and usurpation and so that we would inwardly submit to God's authority without the slightest dissension through our confession that God is the head. We should portray this kind of head covering before the entire creation, especially before the fallen angels (4:9), by confessing God as the head and allowing Him to be the head.

Oh, may we see that God wants the brothers to bare their heads and the sisters to cover theirs in order to obtain a practical portrayal in the universe—especially toward the angels— that we confess God's authority for His glorification and deny Satan's usurpation to his shame. If the brothers do not portray the head and instead say, "Why should we act as the head?" and if the sisters do not cover their head and instead say, "Why should we cover our heads? Why should we submit?" we would be invisibly overthrowing God's arrangement for us, denying His authority, and making Satan with his angels happy. This must be something that the lovers of the Lord would never wish to do. If we truly love the Lord and see this matter, we should willingly submit to God's arrangement, stand in our proper position, and portray the role that God has given us.

Based on Human Nature

1. "Judge this in your own selves: Is it fitting for a woman to pray uncovered to God? Does not even nature itself teach you that if a man has long hair, it is a dishonor to him, but if a woman has long hair, it is a glory to her, because her long hair has been given to her for a covering" (1 Cor. 11:13-15).

The preceding four points of the apostle's teaching concerning head covering are extremely important, but they are based on matters outside of us. However, he also provides a fifth basis for this teaching, which is the human nature inside of us. Our inward human nature tells us that males and females are different; males should bare their heads, and females should hide theirs. I believe that within each one of us there is the feeling that men should be more exposed and women should be more hidden. Therefore, if we are willing to judge according to our inward feeling, our nature will instruct us that it is proper for men to bare their heads and for women to cover theirs.

Our nature was created by God. God's creation is according to His arrangement. His arrangement is for men to be the head and for women to cover their heads. Thus, He created men and women with different natures. These natures cause men to bare their heads, to be the head, and women to cover their heads in submission. This is not a matter of men and women being unequal; rather, it is a matter of men and women having different natures. Since their natures are different, their functions are also different; since their functions are different, their positions are also different. We should not bring in the thought of inequality simply because there are different positions. The stones and wood used in building a house have different natures and thus have different functions and different positions in the building. We should not say that simply because wood is on top of the stones, the two materials are unequal. May we see that our nature causes us to have a different function and position and that we must remain in our own position to exercise our own function for the sake of expressing God's authority and glory.

The points upon which the apostle bases his teaching of head covering are both weighty and deep. These points are not comparable to human ordinances or the customs of a certain time period. God being the head is an honorable and glorious matter. God's arrangement for men and women and His order in creation are holy and eternal. For the sake of angels it is important. The instruction from human nature is deep and intrinsic. These are the bases for the apostle's teaching of head covering and for our practice of head covering.

THE PERSONS COVERING THEIR HEADS

Women Praying or Prophesying

1. "Every woman praying or prophesying with her head uncovered disgraces her head" (1 Cor. 11:5).

Women who are praying or prophesying need to practice head covering because a woman represents submission to authority on the one hand and touches a spiritual matter by praying or prophesying on the other hand. Thus, in the spiritual realm she needs to portray her role in our confession that God is the head and in our submission to His authority.

THE TIME OF HEAD COVERING

The Time of Prayer or Prophesying

1. "Every woman praying or prophesying with her head uncovered disgraces her head" (1 Cor. 11:5).

Because head covering is for the sake of the angels and influences the spiritual realm, it should be practiced when touching spiritual matters. Praying and prophesying are matters that touch the spiritual realm, so when the sisters pray or prophesy, they should cover their heads. According to this principle, even when the sisters are prophesying or fellowshipping with each other, they should have their heads covered because these matters touch the spiritual realm.

The more the sisters touch spiritual things, the more they will feel the need to cover their heads. The more they pray, or the more thoroughly they pray, the more they will feel that they need to cover their heads. When sisters truly pray, their inward parts beg them to cover their head. Especially in the matter of casting out demons, sisters will inwardly feel the need for head covering because they are touching a spiritual realm. When sisters follow their inward feeling and enter into genuine prayer, they will come to a point at which they must cover their heads. When their prayer touches the spiritual realm, it will cause them to cover their heads. Every woman who prays or prophesies—touching the spiritual realm—should cover her head; this shows that the matter of head covering is not so much before humans and for the sake of humans but before God and the angels and for the sake of the spiritual realm.

THE OBJECT WHICH COVERS THE HEAD

Long Hair Not Replacing an Object Which Covers the Head

1. "With her head uncovered...it is one and the same as she who is shaved. For if a woman is not covered, let her hair also be cut off; but if it is shameful for a woman to have her hair cut off or to be shaved, let her be covered" (1 Cor. 11:5-6).

Some say that if women grow long hair, their heads are covered. According to the Word, however, having long hair and covering one's head are two different matters. The apostle says, "With her head uncovered...is one and the same as she who is shaved." He does not say that not covering her head "is" shaving her head. He says that not covering her head is "one and the same as" shaving her head. A woman who prays or prophesies with her head uncovered, even if she has long hair, is "one and the same as" a woman with her head shaved. From this we can see that not covering the head is different from shaving the head. Thus, covering the head cannot be the same thing as growing long hair.

The apostle then says, "If a woman is not covered, let her hair also be cut off; but if it is shameful for a woman to have her hair cut off or to be shaved, let her be covered." This word shows even more clearly that the head covering spoken of by the apostle and the growing of long hair are not the same thing. If a woman does not cover her head, she should cut her hair, but if it is shameful for a woman to cut her hair, she should be covered. Long hair is a woman's glory and if a woman wants to keep her hair long, she should cover her head. If she does not cover her head, she should cut her long hair. Paul's word is not meant to suggest that growing long hair is the same as covering the head; rather, it means that if a woman wants to have long hair, she should cover her head. Having long hair is not the same as covering the head; long hair requires the head to be covered. Covering the head and having long hair are two different matters. Long hair cannot replace head covering.

Long Hair Being God's Arrangement and Head Covering Being Man's Acceptance

1. **"Her long hair has been given to her for a covering"** (1 Cor. 11:15).

Long hair was created by God. God wants hair to cover a woman's head. Thus, women should wear their hair long. Long hair is a woman's glory and was given to women for a covering. This is God's arrangement.

2. **"If a woman is not covered, let her hair also be cut off; but if it is shameful for a woman to have her hair cut off or to be shaved, let her be covered"** (1 Cor. 11:6).

Long hair was given to women as a covering for their heads; it is natural and according to God's arrangement. However, God wants women under His ordination to take a further practical step to confess Him; He wants them to add a covering on top of the covering of hair that He gave them. The sisters' covering of their heads is a confession of God's ordination; it says Amen to His ordination. God ordained long hair to grow on a woman's head for her covering, but a woman's addition of a practical covering is a confession of this ordination and a silent expression of Amen to Him. If a woman is unwilling to accept God's ordination in this matter and unwilling to say Amen, she should cut off the hair that God ordained to grow on her head. If a woman is not willing to add a head covering to the long hair that God ordained to grow on her head and is unwilling to take this practical step to express her acceptance and confession of His ordination, she should cut off the hair that He ordained and publicly express the fact that she does not accept His ordination in this matter. He does not want anyone to be neutral or lukewarm. If a woman is cold, He wants her to be cold, and if she is hot, He wants her to be hot. He wants her to clearly express her acceptance and confession of His ordination by adding a head covering to her hair or to clearly express her rejection of His ordination by cutting off her hair.

Since a head covering is something added on top of the hair, it has the hair as its base. Thus, a head covering should be large enough to cover the hair and take the area of the hair as its standard; it must cover the area covered by the hair, and it needs only to be that large. As for what it is made of, including color and style, it only needs be simple and appropriate.

THE TYPE OF HEAD COVERING

Rebekah

1. "Rebekah lifted up her eyes; and when she saw Isaac...she took her veil and covered herself" (Gen. 24:64-65).

When Rebekah and Isaac were going to be married, she immediately covered herself when she saw Isaac; that is, she covered her head. This can be considered as a type of head covering. Rebekah covered her head as soon as she encountered Isaac because she was going to marry him, to receive him as her head, and to take him as her head; thus, she covered her head.

It is a wonderful matter that almost every woman covers her head when she is married, regardless of whether she is cultured or barbaric. Some use a very thick covering, and others use a very thin lace veil to cover the head. Many people in today's society, however, do not understand the significance of this. We, however, understand it according to God's Word. The Bible shows that a husband is head of the wife (Eph. 5:23). When a woman marries her husband, she receives him as her head; therefore, during the wedding, she should cover her head to signify that from this time onward she accepts the husband she is marrying as her head and that she is willing to take her husband as her head, to allow him to be the head. She acknowledges that she is not the head and that she should not be the head. Although she and her husband were once two, they are now one flesh, so there cannot be two heads; there can only be one head. This is the reason a woman covers her head and hides it at her wedding, leaving her husband as the one head. Every time we see a wedding, we only see one head; the other is hidden. Although two people are standing, only one head is exposed. From the time of the wedding, there is only one head for the two. If the two heads do not become one in a marriage, the result will not be very blessed. If a wedding does not cause a woman to take a man as her head, the spouses will sow bitter seeds and plant a root of disaster. If, however, a wedding causes the two to become one flesh, there will spontaneously be only one head. This is the meaning of head covering in a wedding ceremony. Although worldly people do not understand the significance of head covering and some even oppose its significance, the practice of head covering at weddings, which spans across most cultures throughout time, has been based on this significance.

The High Priest and the Priests

1. "He placed the turban on his head"; "Bound high hats on them" (Lev. 8:9, 13).

In the Old Testament, when the high priest and the priests went in before God, they covered their heads. The high priest used a turban, and the priests used high hats. When they went in before God, they represented God's people, so they had to cover their heads because God is the head of His people, and His people should take Him as their head. Whereas all the brothers and sisters should take God as their head and cover their heads before Him, the brothers, according to the portrait, represent Christ as the head and thus also represent God as the head; consequently, they should not cover their heads.

THE RELATIONSHIP BETWEEN HEAD COVERING
AND THE BREAKING OF BREAD

Head Covering Being Related to the Head
and the Breaking of Bread Being
Related to the Body

1. "Christ is the head"; "Discern the body" (1 Cor. 11:3, 29).

It is really marvelous that the apostle connects the matters of head covering and the breaking of bread. In the first half of 1 Corinthians 11 he teaches head covering, and in the second half he teaches the breaking of bread. When he teaches about head covering, he emphasizes the Head (Christ), and when he teaches about the breaking of bread, he emphasized the Body (the church). Thus, head covering and the breaking of bread are connected; they are the complete story of the Head and the Body. If we only emphasize the breaking of bread but neglect head covering, we emphasize the Body and neglect the Head. This is abnormal. But is this not the situation in today's Christianity? Is there not emphasis on the breaking of bread, but the matter of head covering is neglected? We see people everywhere eating the Lord's supper, breaking the bread, but we rarely see the covering of the head. This is not proper. We cannot live in the Body without submitting to the Head, and we cannot receive the life of the Body without submitting to the authority of the Head. This is the reason that the apostle emphasizes both matters. Moreover, he speaks of head covering before discussing the breaking of bread, because the Head comes before the Body.

Head Covering Being a Matter of Authority
and the Breaking of Bread Being a Matter of Life

1. "Submission to authority"; "Bread" (1 Cor. 11:10, 23).

When the apostle teaches about head covering, he speaks of the matter of authority, and when he teaches about the breaking of bread, he speaks of the matter of life, because in the Bible the head refers to authority, and bread refers to life. The Bible often connects the matters of authority and life. For example, the river of water of life (life) proceeds out from the throne (authority) of God and of the Lamb (Rev. 22:1). Aaron's rod (authority) budded (life) (Heb. 9:4). Authority causes people to receive life, and life gives people authority and causes them to submit to authority. These two are mutual causes and mutual results, so they should be connected.

CHAPTER TWENTY

THE BREAKING OF BREAD

 I. The establishment of the breaking of bread:
   A. The One establishing.
   B. The time of establishing.
   C. The purpose for establishing.
 II. The symbols in the breaking of bread:
   A. The bread.
   B. The cup.
 III. The center of the bread-breaking meeting:
   A. Remembering the Lord.
   B. Enjoying the Lord.
 IV. The declaration of the breaking of bread.
 V. The expectation of the breaking of bread.
 VI. The two aspects of the breaking of bread:
   A. The remembrance of the Lord's supper.
   B. The fellowship of the table.
 VII. The fellowship of the breaking of bread:
   A. Fellowship with the Lord.
   B. Fellowship with all the saints.
 VIII. The testimony of the breaking of bread:
   A. The testimony that we are joined to the Lord.
   B. The testimony of the oneness of the church.
 IX. The discernment of the breaking of bread.
 X. The discipline of the breaking of bread.
 XI. The ones breaking bread.
 XII. The time of the breaking of bread.
 XIII. The place of the breaking of bread.
 XIV. After breaking the bread.

To break bread is to eat the Lord's supper. Since this is a great matter in the New Testament, which expresses our relationship with the Lord Jesus and our relationship with the saints, we cannot neglect it.

THE ESTABLISHMENT OF THE BREAKING OF BREAD

The One Establishing

1. "The Lord Jesus" (1 Cor. 11:23-25; see also Luke 22:19-20; Matt. 26:26-29).

The breaking of bread was established by the Lord Jesus; it was not ordained by the apostles. What the Lord established was passed on to us by the apostles. Thus, our breaking of bread is not merely a matter of keeping the teachings of the apostles; it is our receiving of what was ordained and established by the Lord.

The Time of Establishing

1. "In the night in which He was betrayed" (1 Cor. 11:23).

The Lord Jesus established the table in the night in which He was betrayed, that is, after He ate the Passover feast together with His disciples for the last time, which was also His last supper on earth. It was on the evening of the fourteenth day of the first month of the Hebrew calendar (Exo. 12:2-11). The establishing of the breaking of bread at this time is very meaningful.

The Purpose for Establishing

1. To replace the Old Testament Feast of the Passover (Luke 22:14-20; 1 Cor. 5:7).

In the Old Testament the Israelites kept the Feast of the Passover to remember how God saved them in Egypt through the Passover lamb. The lamb typified the Lord Jesus, and its death typified the death of the Lord Jesus. When the Lord Jesus and His disciples ate the Passover for the last time, He was about to be put to death to shed His blood to accomplish the new covenant. Consequently, at this time He established the breaking of bread as a remembrance for those in the New

Testament age to replace the Old Testament Passover. Since He fulfilled the type of the Passover and His death fulfilled the type of the death of the Passover lamb, He abolished the Passover and established the breaking of bread as its replacement. Just as He and His death fulfilled the type of the Passover, His breaking of bread replaced the remembrance of the Passover.

THE SYMBOLS IN THE BREAKING OF BREAD

The Bread

1. "Jesus took bread and blessed it, and He broke it and gave it to the disciples and said, Take, eat; this is My body"; "Which is given for you" (Matt. 26:26; 1 Cor. 11:24).

When the Lord established the breaking of bread, He first broke the bread and gave it to His disciples, telling them to take and eat. He said that it was His body, which was given for them. Therefore, each time we break bread, there is a loaf of bread on the table for everyone to break and eat. According to the Lord's word, the bread is a symbol of His body. His body was given up for us on the cross. Through His death on the cross, He broke His body and distributed it for us to enjoy. Every time we break the bread and eat the broken pieces, we demonstrate and announce that the Lord's body was broken for us and that through His death on the cross, He has become our portion.

Bread in the Bible refers to life. The Lord said that He is the bread of life and the One who gives life to the world (John 6:33-35). Thus, when we speak of bread, we should think of life. The Lord broke His body for us and distributed it to us like bread; this means that He gave up His body so that we could receive His life. Our receiving of His broken body is our partaking of His life. His life was dispensed to us through the breaking of His body. Thus, He distributes His broken body to us as the bread of life as our portion in life for our enjoyment. This is what is signified by the broken bread.

The Bible shows that God's eternal purpose is to dispense the life in His Son, our Lord Jesus Christ, into people. Therefore, through incarnation His life was embodied in the Lord

Jesus, and He came to earth so that men could receive His life (1:4; 10:10). The Lord Jesus wanted people to receive the life of God within Him, so He needed to die in order to release the life of God from His broken body. Through the death of His physical body, He dispensed the divine life within Him to us. This is the main reason for His giving up His body through His death on the cross. This is the reason He first broke the bread and gave it to the disciples. When He established the breaking of bread, He signified that He was giving up His body for us so that the divine life within Him could become our portion. When we see the bread, when we receive the bread, when we touch and break the bread, we should realize and, even more, manifest and declare by faith that the body of the Lord Jesus was broken for us, enabling us to partake of the divine life within Him. The breaking of the bread speaks of this, and we should manifest this to the entire universe each time we break bread.

The Cup

1. "He took a cup and gave thanks, and He gave it to them, saying, Drink of it, all of you, for this is My blood of the covenant, which is being poured out for many for forgiveness of sins"; "This cup is the new covenant established in My blood" (Matt. 26:27-28; 1 Cor. 11:25).

When the Lord established the breaking of bread, He not only broke bread, gave it to the disciples, and told them to take and eat, He also took a cup, gave it to them, and told them to take and drink. He said that the cup was the new covenant established in His blood, which was being poured out for many for forgiveness of sins. Whenever we break bread, there is not only a loaf on the table that is ready to be broken and eaten by all but also a cup ready to be taken and drunk by all. According to the Lord's word, both the bread and the cup are symbols. The bread refers to His body broken for us, and the cup refers to His blood poured out for us. His body was given for us on the cross, and His blood was shed for us on the cross. On the cross, He not only gave His body for us, but He also poured out His blood for us. His giving of His body was to impart life to us so that we could partake of Him; His shedding of His blood was for our redemption so that our sins could be forgiven.

Although the main goal of the Lord's death on the cross was to release, to dispense, His divine life to us, He not only released His life, but He also redeemed us from all our sins. God's eternal purpose is to dispense His life to us, but because of the fall we also are sinners before God. In order for the Lord to give us the divine life, He had to resolve the problem of our sin. Thus, on the one hand, the Lord gave up His body so that we could receive the divine life within Him, and on the other hand, He shed His blood so that our sins could be forgiven. Although the main emphasis of the breaking of bread is to symbolize the life dispensed to us through the giving of His body, the cup also symbolizes our redemption, which was accomplished through the shedding of His blood.

Cup in the Bible signifies a portion. David said, "Jehovah is the portion of my inheritance and of my cup" (Psa. 16:5). Originally, we were evil sinners, and the portion we should have received from God was the cup of His wrath, that is, the suffering of eternal perdition in the lake of fire (Rev. 14:10; 21:8). When the Lord Jesus was crucified, He drank the cup of wrath on our behalf (John 18:11) and received God's righteous judgment for us, tasting all the sufferings of perdition, shedding His blood, redeeming us from our sins, and establishing a new covenant for us in which we are given the cup of salvation as our cup of blessing (Psa. 116:13; 23:5). In this cup of salvation, God Himself and all that He is becomes our portion—our eternal blessing. Because the Lord Jesus accomplished redemption for us, all that God is and has have become the portion of our cup in God's salvation.

Our sins constituted us as sin and sons of wrath before God and kept us far away from Him; we lost God and all that He is and has. The Lord Jesus bore our sins and God's wrath for us. His shed blood redeemed us from our sins and averted God's wrath; through His blood we have the forgiveness of offenses, and we have been bought by Him so that we can obtain God and all that He is and has. The Lord Jesus' blood established a new covenant on our behalf before God. This new covenant is the portion that we receive from God through the blood of the Lord Jesus; hence, it is symbolized by a cup. The Lord Jesus obtained this cup, the portion of the new covenant, with His blood. Therefore, He said, "This cup is the new covenant established in My blood" (1 Cor. 11:25). This shows that His blood obtained more than just a cup of blessing or an ordinary blessing; rather, the cup is a new covenant, and this blessing, ordained by a new covenant, cannot be changed. The cup obtained for us by His blood is a new covenant established in His blood. In this new covenant, God must forgive our sins and dispense Himself and all that He is and has to us because of the blood of Jesus. Thus, the forgiveness of sins and all that God is and has are the portion that we obtain in the new covenant. This portion is the cup obtained for us by the Lord's blood. His blood takes away sins and brings in God and all that He is and has. This is the cup that we drink when we break bread, and this is what is symbolized when we drink the cup.

The wine in the cup symbolizes the Lord's blood. Therefore, the cup not only symbolizes the new covenant established for us by the Lord's blood but also the blood that He shed for us. The cup is the new covenant established by His blood, and it is also the blood He used to establish this covenant. His blood is for the establishment of the new covenant, and it established the new covenant. The cup of the new covenant was obtained by His blood. Consequently, when we drink the cup, we do not say that we are drinking His blood. Rather, we say that we are drinking the cup of the Lord because His blood established the new covenant for us and became a cup as our appointed portion (v. 27). This portion causes us to be forgiven of our sins and to obtain God and all that He is and has.

THE CENTER OF THE BREAD-BREAKING MEETING

Remembering the Lord

1. "The Lord Jesus...took bread...broke it and said... this do unto the remembrance of Me" (1 Cor. 11:23-24).

When we come together to break bread, it is not for the

purpose of praying to receive grace or to hear a message to be edified; rather, it is to remember the Lord. Thus, the nature of the bread-breaking meeting is different from any other meeting. Other meetings, which have prayer, messages, exhortation, and testimonies as their center, are for us to obtain something. In contrast, our remembrance of the Lord is the center of the bread-breaking meeting, and it is for the Lord to obtain something. Therefore, in the bread-breaking meeting all the hymns, the prayers of thanksgiving and praise, the reading of Scripture, or the spiritual speaking should center on the Lord and declare the Lord's person, work, grace, virtues, life and suffering on earth, or honor and glory in the heavens in order that all would remember the Lord Himself. In the bread-breaking meeting, our actions should bring the hearts and minds of everyone to the Lord, causing them to see Him and to offer thanksgiving, praise, worship, and love to Him. In this meeting we should not do anything that would disrupt our thoughts and hearts, causing us to be inwardly unable to turn to the Lord or to focus our thoughts and hearts on Him. In this meeting we should focus on the Lord and behold Him so that we are filled with spiritual feelings about Him, which we can outwardly express in hymns, prayers, Scripture readings, or prophesying, in order to keep the entire attention of the meeting on the Lord Himself and to enable everyone to sense the Lord or some aspect concerning Him in remembrance of Him.

In the bread-breaking meeting, when we see or receive the bread, we should consider how the Lord was incarnated for us, how He died for us in the flesh, and how His body was broken for us and dispensed to us, giving us His life. When we see the bread or receive the bread, we should consider how the bread is made from wheat, which passed through wind and sun, which was ground and baked to become a loaf that could be broken, and which was broken to become the portion that we enjoy. This speaks of the experiences that the Lord passed through for His life to become our enjoyment. Based on the meaning of these symbols, we should consider the sufferings that the Lord experienced on our behalf as our remembrance of the Lord Himself. Before the bread, we should think only of the Lord and all that His love has accomplished for us; we should not think of ourselves or anything concerning ourselves, because we are in a meeting to remember the Lord.

2. "Similarly also the cup...saying...this do, as often as you drink it, unto the remembrance of Me" (1 Cor. 11:25).

In the bread-breaking meeting we should not only think of the Lord and all that He has done for us when we look at the bread and receive it, we should also remember Him when we look at the cup and receive it. When we see the cup and receive it to drink, we should consider how the Lord partook of flesh and blood for us (Heb. 2:14), how He gave up His body for us to obtain His life, and how He shed His blood for us so that we could obtain the highest blessing of being freed from sin and gaining God and all that He is and has. As we drink the cup, we should consider how the grapes went through the process of being crushed in order for their juice to flow out. From the meaning of this symbol, we should consider how the Lord was pressed by God, how He bore our sins and became sin for us, how He was judged in our place, became a curse, and shed His blood to become our cup of blessing as our portion. We should consider how we have redemption, forgiveness of sins, sanctification, justification, reconciliation to God, and acceptance by God through the Lord's blood. We should consider how the blood washes us of our sins, cleanses our conscience, and stops our conscience from condemning us, enabling us to boldly approach God without fear. We should consider how it argues before God on our behalf, speaks better words for us, defends us against the attack of evil spirits, and causes us to overcome our accuser Satan. We should think only of His love, His sufferings, and His accomplishments in the shedding of His blood for us. We should not think of our sins and offenses when we see the cup, which symbolizes the Lord's blood. The cup that we drink should cause us to remember the Lord and to think of His accomplishments in the shedding of His blood for us; its purpose is not related to the remembrance of our sins, offenses, and trespasses.

Enjoying the Lord

1. "Jesus took bread...and He broke it and gave it to the disciples and said, Take, eat"; "This is My body which is being given for you; do this in remembrance of Me"; "And He took a cup...and He gave it to them, saying, Drink of it, all of you, for this is My blood"; "Which is being poured out for you"; "This do, as often as you drink it, unto the remembrance of Me" (Matt. 26:26; Luke 22:19; Matt. 26:27-28; Luke 22:20; 1 Cor. 11:25).

Although the center of the bread-breaking meeting is our remembrance of the Lord, our remembrance is not merely to think about the Lord and all that He accomplished for us but also to enjoy the Lord and all that He accomplished for us. The Lord said that eating the bread and drinking the cup are a remembrance of Him. The bread and the cup symbolize His body and His blood. Thus, eating the bread and drinking the cup symbolize our eating of His body and our drinking of His blood. His body and blood, which were given for us, are the means by which He accomplished everything for us. However, eating and drinking involve more than just receiving; there is also enjoyment. When we eat the Lord's body and drink the Lord's blood, we are not only receiving but also enjoying Him and all that He accomplished by giving His body and shedding His blood for us. This is our remembrance of Him. Our remembrance of Him through the breaking of bread is not only objective; it is not a remembrance of someone who is outside of us and far away from us but a subjective remembrance of the Lord whom we have received into us as our enjoyment.

When people in the world remember someone, they can only think about a person, including his kindness, good deeds, and notable achievements. But when we remember the Lord, we do not merely think about the Lord's grace, love, virtues, honor, glory, and marvelous works; we actually receive and enjoy Him and all that He is and has. People in the world can only remember those who are far away; they cannot receive the ones whom they remember into themselves as their enjoyment. But we can do more than simply remember a person who is no longer with us; we can receive the Lord into us as our life supply and as the enjoyment of our heart.

Whenever we break bread to remember the Lord, we should not just quietly think about the Lord's person and work; we should offer up praises and thanksgiving, opening our spirits to receive the Lord and all that He is and has as our inward enjoyment. The more we enjoy the Lord, the more we remember Him. The true meaning of remembering the Lord is enjoyment. When we break bread, we inwardly receive the Lord and all that He is and has as our enjoyment. This is our true remembrance of Him.

THE DECLARATION OF THE BREAKING OF BREAD

1. "As often as you eat this bread and drink the cup, you declare the Lord's death until He comes" (1 Cor. 11:26).

The word *declare* means "display" in the original Greek. The apostle said that every time we eat the bread and drink the cup, we display the Lord's death. This means that we display His death for all to see. The bread symbolizes His body, and the cup symbolizes His blood. The cup placed beside the bread indicates that the Lord's blood is outside of His body because it flowed out of His body and has been separated from His body. A person dies when his blood is separated from his body. Therefore, when we break bread and place the cup beside the bread, it displays the Lord's death by spreading out His death before the universe for God, the angels, Satan, the demons, and all creation, including us, to see. (This is the reason that the bread and cup should not be covered by a cloth.) Every time we see the bread and cup, we see a display of the Lord's death. Although we break the bread in remembrance of the Lord, we also display His death. During the bread-breaking meeting our hearts remember the Lord, our spirits enjoy the Lord, and our eyes should look upon His death.

The Lord's death is the center of His work of redemption. The Lord's redemptive work was accomplished through and is based upon His death. His death solves the problem of sin, satisfies the requirements of the law, and quells God's righteous wrath, causing us to be reconciled and acceptable to

God. The Lord's death resolves the problems of the old man, the flesh, and the old creation, delivering us from sin, the law, and all the bondage and slavery of the old creation. His death also solves the problem of the devil, Satan, and the world, causing us to boast in triumph over him. The Lord's death is all-inclusive. Everything that is opposed to God, incompatible with God, apart from God, or not of God, including sin, the flesh, Satan, the world, and the old creation, was terminated in this death. When we break bread by placing the bread and cup separately on the table, we display to the universe the all-inclusive death of the Lord which solved all the problems between us and God. As we display the Lord's death, we also display everything that the Lord accomplished through His death to God, to the created things in the universe, and to ourselves.

THE EXPECTATION OF THE BREAKING OF BREAD

1. "Until He comes" (1 Cor. 11:26).

When we break bread, we not only remember and declare but also expect. Our remembrance is to remember the Lord Himself, to enjoy Him; our declaration is to declare the Lord's death, to display His death; and our expectation is to expect the Lord's return, to wait for His return. When we break bread, on the one hand, we should remember the Lord Himself and contact Him, and on the other hand, we should contemplate the Lord's death and await the Lord's coming. We remember Him because He left and went into the heavens. But He promised that He would come from the heavens to receive us, so we also wait for Him. With respect to our remembrance, He is not visibly with us; with respect to our expectation, He will visibly come again to be with us. Even though He is the Spirit who is invisible but inwardly with us, we must wait for His second coming in order to have His visible, outward presence. When we break bread, we can touch His inward, invisible presence, but we hope even more for His outward, visible presence. His invisible presence causes us to thirst for His visible presence. Thus, when we break bread, we enjoy His invisible presence and we look forward to His visible presence. We contact Him while waiting for Him to come again.

THE TWO ASPECTS OF THE BREAKING OF BREAD

The Remembrance of the Lord's Supper

1. "Eat the Lord's supper"; "This do...unto the remembrance of Me" (1 Cor. 11:20, 25).

Breaking bread has two significant aspects. The first aspect of eating the Lord's supper is our remembrance of Him. In this aspect, we remember the Lord by eating the bread and drinking the cup, we display His death, and we await His coming. This speaks of our relationship with the Lord. This aspect of bread breaking is emphasized in 1 Corinthians 11.

The Fellowship of the Table

1. "Partake of the Lord's table"; "The fellowship of the blood of Christ...the fellowship of the body of Christ" (1 Cor. 10:21, 16).

The second aspect of bread breaking is to partake of the Lord's table and to have fellowship with all the saints. When we partake of the Lord's table together with all the saints, we receive the Lord's body and blood, and through them we have fellowship. In this aspect the Lord's body and blood become our enjoyment with all the saints, and they are our fellowship with all the saints. This speaks of our relationship with all the saints. This aspect of bread breaking is emphasized in 1 Corinthians 10.

When we break bread, we eat the Lord's supper on the one hand, and we partake of the Lord's table on the other hand. The Lord's supper is our remembrance of the Lord; it is a matter between the Lord and us, and it speaks of the love between the Lord and us. The Lord's table is our fellowship with all the saints; it is a matter between all the saints, and it speaks of our fellowship with all the saints. We will speak in more detail concerning this fellowship in the following points.

THE FELLOWSHIP OF THE BREAKING OF BREAD

Fellowship with the Lord

1. "Jesus took bread and blessed it, and He broke it and gave it to the disciples and said, Take, eat"; "This is My body which is being given for you"; "And He took

a cup and gave thanks, and He gave it to them, saying, Drink of it, all of you, for this is My blood"; "Which is being poured out for you" (Matt. 26:26; Luke 22:19; Matt. 26:27-28; Luke 22:20).

When we break bread, the Lord gives us the bread and the cup; as we receive the bread and the cup from Him, we have fellowship with Him, and He has fellowship with us. He gives the bread and the cup to us; that is, He gives us His body and His blood, which means He gives Himself to us in fellowship. We receive the bread and the cup from Him; that is, we receive His body and His blood, which means we receive Him personally and thus have fellowship with Him. He gives His body and His blood to us in fellowship, and through His body given for us and His blood poured out for us, He gives Himself to us in fellowship for our enjoyment. We receive His body and His blood through His body given for us and His blood poured out for us, and we enjoy Him and have fellowship with Him.

Fellowship is communion, even an intimate communication, between two parties; therefore, in order for two parties to have fellowship with one another, they must have the same life and nature. The Lord Jesus was incarnated to put on our nature and to become the same as we; He gave up His body for us so that we could have His life and become the same as He is. His incarnation and His giving up of His body caused Him and us, us and Him, to have the same life and nature. Even though He is God, He has the human life and nature; even though we are men, we have God's divine life and nature. Thus, He and we, we and He, have the same life and nature. In this same life and nature, we and He, He and we, can have fellowship and intimate communication with each other. Despite the fact that we were originally full of sin and could not contact Him as the sinless One, He shed His blood and fully redeemed us from our sins, causing us to become as sinless as He is; thus, we can contact Him and have fellowship with Him.

Because the Lord gave up His body and poured out His blood to enable us to have fellowship with Him, His body and His blood have become the factors of our fellowship with Him.

We fellowship with Him through His body and His blood, and in this fellowship with Him, we enjoy His body and blood. His body and blood enable us to have fellowship with Him; they are the fellowship between us and Him. In this fellowship we contact Him through His body and blood, and we receive everything that He accomplished through the giving up of His body and the pouring out of His blood as our enjoyment.

Fellowship with All the Saints

1. "The cup of blessing which we bless, is it not the fellowship of the blood of Christ? The bread which we break, is it not the fellowship of the body of Christ?" (1 Cor. 10:16).

This verse speaks not only of our fellowship with the Lord through His blood and body but even more of our fellowship in the Lord's blood and body with all the saints. We have fellowship with the Lord when we enjoy the Lord's blood and body by drinking the cup and eating the bread. But we do not drink the cup and eat the bread individually, and we do not enjoy the Lord's blood and body by ourselves. Rather, we eat, drink, and enjoy with all the saints. We drink the Lord's cup as our corporate enjoyment of the Lord's blood together with all the saints, and we eat the Lord's bread as our corporate enjoyment of the Lord's body together with all the saints. Thus, when we drink the cup and eat the bread, we have fellowship in the Lord's blood and body with all the saints. The cup and bread enter into us, and they enter into every one of the saints. Every saint partakes of the cup and the bread, so we all partake of His blood and body; that is, we all receive the redemption accomplished by the pouring out of His blood and the life dispensed by the giving up of His body. The Lord's blood and body are the common portion that we enjoy with all the saints, and this portion causes us to have fellowship with all the saints. In fact, it is the very fellowship that we have with all the saints. This is why the cup that we drink is the fellowship of the Lord's blood, and the bread that we eat is the fellowship of the Lord's body. Every time we drink the cup and eat the bread, all the saints have fellowship in the Lord's blood and body. Therefore, our bread breaking is not merely a remembrance of the Lord, an enjoyment of the Lord, or a fellowship with the Lord but also a fellowship with all the saints. It is not merely a matter between us and the Lord; it is also a matter among all the saints. If our breaking of bread does not cause us to have fellowship with all the saints, if it does not speak forth our relationship with all the saints, it is improper and problematic.

THE TESTIMONY OF THE BREAKING OF BREAD

The Testimony That We Are Joined to the Lord

1. "Jesus took bread and...gave it to the disciples and said, Take, eat; this is My body. And He took a cup...and He gave it to them, saying, Drink of it, all of you, for this is My blood" (Matt. 26:26-28).

When we break bread, the Lord gives us the bread and the cup and tells us to take and to eat and drink. He wants us to receive His body and blood as our enjoyment. This speaks of our being joined to the Lord, and it testifies that we are joined to the Lord. When we eat the bread and drink the cup, we take them into us, signifying that, through the Lord's giving up of His body and the pouring out of His blood, He came into us and joined Himself to us. When we receive the Lord's body given for us and His blood poured out for us, we also testify that we have partaken of both Him and His accomplishments for us and thus are joined with Him. Every time we break bread, we testify that we and He, He and we, have been joined as one because of the redemption accomplished through the Lord's giving up of His body and the shedding of His blood. We are now in Him, and He is now in us. The bread that we break testifies that His life was released to become our life. As we break the bread, we testify that we have obtained His life and are joined to Him in life because of what He accomplished by giving up His body and being broken for us. The cup that we drink testifies that we are worthy to be joined to Him because His blood was poured out to expunge our sins. As we drink the cup, we testify that we have obtained His life and are worthy to be joined to Him in life because of the redemption accomplished by the shedding of His blood.

The Testimony of the Oneness of the Church

1. **"We who are many are one Body; for we all partake of the one bread"** (1 Cor. 10:17).

When we break bread, not only do we testify that we are joined to the Lord, but we also testify that we are joined to all the saints and are in oneness with all the saints; that is, we are in the oneness of the church. This is testified by the breaking of bread as it relates to the Lord's table. The breaking of bread as it relates to the Lord's supper refers to the Lord's *own* body (His body of flesh) and signifies that the Lord's own body was broken for us; the breaking of bread as it relates to Lord's table refers to the Lord's *mystical* Body (the church) and signifies that the Lord's mystical Body is one. The Lord gave up His physical body to produce His mystical Body. He is the grain of wheat who produced many grains through death and resurrection to form the many grains into one loaf (John 12:24), which is the one Body. The many grains are those who have obtained His life in every time and every place. As the many grains, we are not scattered; rather, in the Holy Spirit, we are one bread, one Body (1 Cor. 12:13). Although we are many grains with life, many people with life, we do not exist individually, grain by grain or one by one; instead, all of us have become one bread, one Body. Therefore, the apostle says, "We who are many are one Body."

Thus, the bread that we break in the aspect of the Lord's table refers to the entire Body of Christ, including all the saved ones in every time and every place. Peter and Paul are in this bread; Martin Luther, J. N. Darby, George Müller, D. L. Moody, all of us who are saved today, and all those who will be saved in the future are in this one bread. All the saved ones, whether in the past, in the present, or in the future, are in this one bread, and all partake of this one bread.

Therefore, when we break bread, on the one hand, we testify that we are one with the Lord, and on the other hand, we testify that we are also one with all the saints, that is, with all the saved ones in every time and every place. We and all the saved ones in every time and every place are one in the Lord's life, that is, are one Body. All those with the Lord's life in every time and every place participate in the Lord's mystical Body, are one in His life, and have become one Body. This is what the bread that we break and eat signifies in relation to the Lord's table, and this is our testimony when we break the bread in this aspect. Therefore, the bread that we break signifies not only the Lord's own body but all the saints in every time and every place. We must not break bread only to remember the Lord and display His death; we must also testify that we are one with all the saints in every time and every place. We and all the saints in every time and every place partake of this one bread. Although we are all in different times and different places when we break the bread, we all still break this one bread. In the past Peter and Paul broke this one bread; today we are breaking this one bread. The brothers in China break this one bread, and the brothers in other countries break this one bread. It does not matter that we are in different times or places when we break the bread; we all break one bread because we all belong to this one loaf, and we are all part of the one Body represented by this bread.

The bread that we break represents the one Body of Christ in the universe, so the bread that we break in every time and every place is a representation of the one bread, the one Body. The bread that we broke last year, the bread broken this year, the bread broken last Lord's Day, the bread broken this Lord's Day, the bread broken in Taipei, the bread broken in Kaohsiung, the bread broken in Hall 1, and the bread broken in Hall 5 are all the one bread which symbolizes the one Body. In the universe there is only the one Body of Christ, and this Body is one. Our breaking of only one bread testifies to this fact.

THE DISCERNMENT OF THE BREAKING OF BREAD

With the degradation of the church, the matter of bread breaking became confused; therefore, the Holy Spirit in the Bible teaches us to have discernment concerning the breaking of bread.

1. "You come together not for the better but for the worse. For first of all, when you come together in the church, I hear that divisions exist among you" (1 Cor. 11:17-18).

According to verse 20, the coming together spoken of in verses 17 and 18 is the bread-breaking meeting. Some bread-breaking meetings were not for the better but for the worse because divisions existed among those attending the meeting. *First of all* refers to the main reason. When the believers meet together to break bread, they testify of the oneness of Christ's Body, the church. If those who meet together to break bread have divisions among themselves, or if a bread-breaking meeting is on a sectarian ground instead of the ground of the oneness of the church, the meeting will not match the essential oneness of the church, and it will damage the oneness of the church. Consequently, the attendants of such a meeting will come together for the worse and will suffer loss. Every time we attend a meeting to break bread, we must discern its ground to determine whether it is a meeting in division or in oneness. Is it a sect, or is it the church? We must discern whether the meeting has a divisive element or a sectarian factor lest we come together for the worse and suffer a loss.

2. "When therefore you come together in the same place, it is not to eat the Lord's supper; for in your eating, each one takes his own supper first, and one is hungry and the other is drunk" (1 Cor. 11:20-21).

Here the apostle warns us that some bread-breaking meetings are not to eat the Lord's supper. *When therefore...it is not* refers to the divisions mentioned in the preceding verses. A divisive bread-breaking meeting, that is, a sectarian bread-breaking meeting, in the apostle's eyes and in the Lord's eyes is not the Lord's supper. The bread broken in the Lord's supper symbolizes the entire Body of Christ and testifies to the oneness of the Body of Christ, the church. If bread is broken on a sectarian, divisive ground, or if bread with a divisive, sectarian element is broken, it does not correspond with the element of the oneness of the church, and it loses the testimony and significance of bread breaking. Therefore, "it is not" bread breaking.

Christ is not divided (1:13); the church is one (12:13). Thus, in the church those who belong to Christ should not be divided or divide into sects, saying, "I am of such-and-such a church" or "I am of such-and-such a group" (cf. 1:10-12). When the believers break bread, they testify that the church is one on the positive side, and they simultaneously announce that there is no room for divisions and sects on the negative side. Yet some bread is broken on a sectarian ground with the element of division in it. Thus, it is no wonder that through the apostle the Holy Spirit declares that this kind of bread breaking is not the Lord's supper.

Another reason that some bread breaking is not the Lord's supper is that some mix this matter with their own supper and make it common. This was the practice of the Corinthians in Paul's time. On the one hand, they ate the Lord's supper, and on the other, they ate their own supper. The poor among them went hungry while the rich were drunk with wine. In doing this, they confused the special characteristic of the Lord's supper and lost the significance of bread breaking. Consequently, it was not to eat the Lord's supper or to break bread. We cannot eat the Lord's supper as if it were an ordinary meal or consider the breaking of bread to be a common thing. We must preserve the holy nature of the Lord's supper, and we must honor the high significance of the breaking of bread; otherwise, we will change the nature of the Lord's supper, causing it to equal nothing and become a matter of loss rather than profit.

3. "Whoever eats the bread or drinks the cup of the Lord in an unworthy manner will be guilty of the body and of the blood of the Lord" (1 Cor. 11:27).

According to the apostle's word, it is possible for people to break bread in an unworthy manner. The unworthiness spoken of in this verse includes at least the two matters which were previously mentioned: divisions and treating the Lord's supper as something common. Whoever is in division or treats the Lord's supper as something common breaks bread in an unworthy manner. This kind of bread breaking makes one guilty of the body and of the blood of the Lord. The Lord's body was given for us so that we could receive His life and become

His mystical Body, and the Lord's blood was poured out for us to make us worthy to receive His life to become His mystical Body. This is the testimony signified by our eating the bread and drinking the cup. If we break bread in division on a sectarian ground, we bring the element of division into our breaking of bread and damage the testimony of the oneness of His mystical Body, the church. If we treat His supper as common, we annul the special significance of His body which was given for us and of His blood which was poured out for us. Thus, we are guilty of His body and His blood. We should not do this!

In verse 26 the apostle says that the breaking of bread is to remember the Lord through enjoying the bread and the cup and to declare His death as we await His return. Thus, to eat the bread or drink the cup of the Lord in an unworthy manner, as spoken of in verse 27, includes not practicing the fellowship of the apostle in the preceding verse. If, in our breaking of bread, we do not enjoy Him, remember Him, display His death, or wait for His coming, we are eating His bread and drinking His cup in an unworthy manner. A nominal Christian without the Lord's life or an unsaved false believer cannot remember the Lord, display His death, or await His coming, so if such a person eats the Lord's bread and drinks His cup, he is unworthy and is guilty of His body and blood. We should not do this either.

4. "Let a man prove himself, and in this way let him eat of the bread and drink of the cup. For he who eats and drinks, eats and drinks judgment to himself if he does not discern the body" (1 Cor. 11:28-29).

Because there is the possibility of breaking bread in an unworthy manner and thus being guilty of the Lord's body and blood, we must take the responsibility to prove ourselves and to discern whenever we break bread. To prove is to examine the bread to see whether it is a bread of division, of a sectarian nature, or with a divisive element. Does the bread-breaking meeting treat the Lord's supper as a common thing? Does it respect the honorable significance of bread breaking? To prove is to examine the ground, nature, and element of the bread-breaking meeting; it is also to prove our own individual motive and condition in a self-examination. Are we personally divisive in the church? Do we have a sectarian element? Are we one with the brothers and sisters? Are we treating the meeting as common and unimportant? Is our living up to the standard and worthy of the testimony of the breaking of bread? To discern is to test the bread to see whether it refers both to the Lord's body given for us and to His mystical Body. Does it represent the Body of Christ—the church? Does it testify to the oneness of the church? Does it prove that "we who are many are one Body; for we all partake of the one bread" (10:17)? Does it represent some sect or denomination, or does it represent the unique church? After we discern that the bread represents the Body of Christ and decide to break the bread, we must also prove ourselves to see whether we have any disagreement, dispute, or problem with any saint who is a member with us. Are we jealous; do we dislike or despise certain brothers and sisters? We must prove and discern. We must know that the bread is not a bread of division, that the meeting is not treating the Lord's supper as something common, that we ourselves are not divisive, that we are not in disagreement with the brothers and sisters, and that we are not taking the Lord's supper lightly and eating it loosely. We also must know that the bread represents the Body of Christ and testifies to the oneness of the church. Furthermore, we must see whether we have any problems or disaccord with any saint who is a member together with us. There cannot be any separation between members. Everything must be so clear before we eat the bread and drink the cup. If we are not in such a clear condition, we are guilty of the body of the Lord and of His blood, and we eat and drink judgment to ourselves. *Eats and drinks judgment to himself* means that the eating and drinking cause one to be judged and condemned. Therefore, if we do not prove and discern according to the foregoing matters, breaking bread will cause us to be judged and condemned; it will cause us to suffer loss. We must be careful about this matter.

5. "If we discerned ourselves, we would not be judged"; "Not come together for judgment" (1 Cor. 11:31, 34).

Come together for judgment in the original Greek means "come together and bring judgment upon ourselves." The meeting spoken of here is the bread-breaking meeting. Thus, these verses tell us that the bread-breaking meeting can cause us to be judged and condemned. Consequently, whenever we break bread, we first must discern clearly and prove ourselves thoroughly. If we do this, we will not be judged, and we will not bring judgment upon ourselves. We will not be condemned and suffer loss. Therefore, in the matter of breaking bread we must discern and prove ourselves.

THE DISCIPLINE OF THE BREAKING OF BREAD

1. "Come together...for the worse"; "Come together for judgment" (1 Cor. 11:17, 34).

If we do not eat the bread and drink the cup in an approved manner when we come together to break bread, we are guilty of the body and the blood of the Lord. This is to come together for the worse, and it brings judgment and condemnation upon ourselves. If we have a divisive element, if we break bread on a sectarian ground, or if we treat the Lord's supper as a common meal when we break bread, we bring condemnation and judgment upon ourselves and will be disciplined.

2. "Eats and drinks judgment to himself" (1 Cor. 11:29).

If we do not discern whether the bread we break represents the Lord's physical body given up for His mystical Body, if we do not discern whether the bread represents the entire Body of Christ, the whole church, and if we break bread loosely, we eat and drink condemnation and judgment to ourselves. This will cause us to be condemned and disciplined.

3. "Because of this many among you are weak and sick, and a number sleep" (1 Cor. 11:30).

Because the Corinthian believers did not break bread in an approved manner by proving or discerning themselves, they brought discipline onto themselves. This discipline caused many of them to be weak and sick, and a number even died. Since some did not eat the bread and drink the cup in an approved manner, the Lord caused them to become physically weak as a warning. When they disregarded the warning of their physical weakness and continued to be guilty of the Lord's body and blood, He gave a stronger warning by allowing some to become physically sick. When they disregarded the stronger warning of their physical sickness without proving and discerning themselves, there was a final discipline of death. This is very serious. This should be a warning to all of us. Is it not possible that the weakness, sickness, and even death of many believers is due to their breaking of the bread in a disapproved manner, without proving or discerning themselves and thus being guilty of the Lord's body and blood? Could it not be that they are eating and drinking judgment, condemnation, and discipline to themselves? May the brothers and sisters who are weak, sick, and even dying seek the Lord's enlightenment in this matter, receive the Lord's warning, and be adjusted in their way of breaking bread so that they may be spared the discipline of judgment. May all of us who have received the Lord's grace prove ourselves and solemnly discern the matter of breaking bread lest we come into judgment and are disciplined by the Lord.

THE ONES BREAKING BREAD

1. "Gave it to the disciples" (Matt. 26:26).

When the Lord established the matter of bread breaking, He gave the bread and cup to His disciples. The disciples, who received the Lord's salvation and life, belonged to the Lord. Only those who have this kind of relationship with the Lord and who know the Lord as their salvation can remember the Lord and declare His death through the bread and the cup. How can those who have not received the Lord's salvation, who have not been brought into a life relationship with the Lord in His salvation, remember the Lord? How can those who have not received the redemption accomplished by the Lord's giving up of His body and shedding of His blood declare His death through the bread and the cup? Those who are not saved cannot and should not break bread. Nominal Christians, who have only been ritually baptized without obtaining the Lord's life, and false believers, who have only a name but not the reality, cannot and should not break bread.

Some think that Judas was present when the Lord established the breaking of bread. This is not so. In the four Gospels, Matthew, Mark, and John all tell us that Judas, who betrayed the Lord, left before the Lord established His supper (Matt. 26:17-28; Mark 14:17-24; John 13:2, 21-30). Only Luke is different (22:14-23). This is because Luke's record is according to the order of morality, but Matthew, Mark, and John are according to the order of history. All the authoritative Bible expositors attest to this. Before the establishment of the breaking of bread, Judas left. How could the Lord require one to remember Him who had not received Him as Savior, who did not have a relationship with Him in His salvation? Therefore, only those who have received the Lord's salvation, who have the Lord's life, and who belong to the Lord are able and qualified to break bread in remembrance of the Lord.

2. **"All those who believed...breaking bread"** (Acts 2:44, 46).

Those who break bread should be those who believe. The believers are those who have received the Lord's salvation through faith, partake of His life, and belong to Him. Only those who have this kind of faith are able and permitted to break bread.

THE TIME OF THE BREAKING OF BREAD

1. **"Continued steadfastly...in the breaking of bread"** (Acts 2:42).

The early believers continued steadfastly in the breaking of bread. *Continued steadfastly* in the original Greek denotes "continued without ceasing," which means "always." Always breaking bread is the pattern that the early believers left for us, and we should follow them.

2. **"Day by day...breaking bread"** (Acts 2:46).

The early believers continued steadfastly in breaking bread to such an extent that they broke bread day by day. At that time the believers were on fire for the Lord and loved Him deeply; therefore, they spontaneously wanted to break bread day by day in remembrance of Him. This tells us that the more often we break bread to remember the Lord, the better.

3. "On the first day of the week...gathered together to break bread" (Acts 20:7).

At first, the early believers broke bread day by day, but later as it became a long-term practice, they broke bread once a week on the first day of the week. The first day of the week is the Lord's Day, the day of the Lord's resurrection; it is also the beginning of the week, which symbolizes that old things have passed away and a new life has begun. Breaking bread in remembrance of the Lord on this day is most appropriate because even though we break bread to declare the Lord's death, we remember Him in resurrection. We break bread in the realm of resurrection, and we remember the Lord based on the life of the new creation. Thus, it is not only a convenient time but also very meaningful to come together to remember the Lord on the day in which old things passed away and new life began, the day of the Lord's resurrection.

4. "Supper" (1 Cor. 11:20).

Since breaking bread is to eat the Lord's supper, it is best that it is held in the evening in order to fit the name. Moreover, in the evening all the things of the day are finished and our personal burdens are laid aside, so our hearts are light and our spirits are happy. This is the most appropriate attitude in which to remember the Lord and to sense His presence as we touch Him. This, however, is not a law. If it is too difficult to arrange the meeting in the evening, or if it is not convenient, we can do what is convenient and hold the meeting in the morning or at midday.

THE PLACE OF THE BREAKING OF BREAD

1. "Breaking bread from house to house" (Acts 2:46).

The earliest believers broke bread in many of the believers' homes. At that time there were many people, so it would have been inconvenient with regard to both time and space for them to gather together to break bread in one place; therefore, they spontaneously split up into different homes for this practice. This shows that if there are many believers in one place, they may divide themselves among different homes to break bread.

296 CRUCIAL TRUTHS IN THE HOLY SCRIPTURES

2. "When therefore you come together in the same place...to eat the Lord's supper" (1 Cor. 11:20).

It is permissible for the believers in one locality to divide themselves among homes and break bread, but it is more appropriate and more flavorful if everyone can come together in the same place to break bread. Thus, the early believers came together in the same place to eat the Lord's supper. Today when we break bread, we may either split up or all come together as best fits our need.

AFTER BREAKING THE BREAD

1. "As often as you eat this bread and drink the cup, you declare the Lord's death until He comes" (1 Cor. 11:26).

Those who break bread in remembrance of the Lord should long for the Lord and await His coming. Therefore, after we break bread, we should long for the Lord's appearing and live a life of waiting for the Lord. If we only break bread in remembrance of the Lord every week but do not live a life of desiring His coming and waiting for Him, we are not in accordance with the meaning of breaking bread.

2. "You cannot drink the Lord's cup and the demons' cup; you cannot partake of the Lord's table and of the demons' table" (1 Cor. 10:21).

After partaking of the Lord's table, we cannot partake of the demons' table; after drinking the Lord's cup, we cannot drink the demons' cup. According to the preceding verses, the demons' table and the demons' cup refer to the things sacrificed to idols. After breaking bread, we cannot eat anything sacrificed to an idol. When we break bread, we fellowship with the Lord, just as when Gentiles worship idols, they fellowship with the demons. After we fellowship with the Lord, how can we return to partake of something related to fellowship with demons? Therefore, after breaking the Lord's bread, we cannot return to eating idol sacrifices.

The demons' table and the demons' cup refer to idol sacrifices. But is not worldly enjoyment also a demons' table? Is not worldly prosperity a demons' cup? Since we have enjoyed the Lord Himself and all that He is and has at His table, how can we go back to desire worldly pleasures? Since we have been satisfied by the Lord at His table, how can we go back to Satan to obtain anything? How can we return to Satan's world to obtain the pleasure that Satan gives to people? After breaking bread, we should not lust after the world and its enjoyment.

3. "Let us keep the feast, not with old leaven, neither with the leaven of malice and evil, but with the unleavened bread of sincerity and truth" (1 Cor. 5:8).

In the time of the Old Testament, the Israelites kept the Feast of the Passover and immediately followed it with the Feast of Unleavened Bread, during which they eliminated every bit of leaven from their lives (Deut. 16:1-4). Since the breaking of bread in the New Testament replaced the Passover in the Old Testament, we should be like the Israelites after the Passover and eliminate all leaven from our lives. Leaven refers to all evil and malice, to all things that can corrupt man. After breaking bread we should remove all sin, evil, and every corrupting thing from our lives, and we should no longer keep the old living that we had before we were saved. We should not have any of our former evil, our old leaven; rather, we should live a holy, sinless life by the Lord's holy, sinless life, that is, by the unleavened bread of sincerity and truth. We should truly be those who keep the Feast of Unleavened Bread so that we can be those who are entirely according to the breaking of bread.

CHAPTER TWENTY-ONE

OBEYING THE SENSE OF LIFE

I. Believers having the sense of life once they are saved:
   A. The light of life.
   B. The law of God written on our hearts.
   C. The law of the Spirit of life.
   D. God operating in us.
   E. Christ living in us.
   F. The teaching of the anointing.

II. The sense of life:
   A. When the light of life shines within us, we have an inward sense, and what we sense within is our inward seeing.
   B. When the law of God, the law of the Spirit of life, functions within us, it gives us an inward sense.
   C. The operation of God with us also gives us a sense of life.
   D. Christ in us is not only alive but also living, so we have an inward sense of Him.
   E. Having an inward sense of the teaching of the anointing within us because the anointing of the ointment is the speaking and the shining of the revelation of the Holy Spirit within us.

III. The responsibility of the believers toward the sense of life:
   A. Walking according to the Spirit—setting the mind on the Spirit.
   B. Caring for the sense of life and peace.
   C. Obeying with fear and trembling.
   D. Fellowshipping with the Lord according to the teaching of the anointing.

IV. The maintenance, recovery, and increase of the sense of life.

V. The result of the believers' obeying the sense of life:
   A. Sensing life and peace.
   B. Abiding in the Lord.
   C. Working out our salvation.
   D. Accomplishing the good pleasure of God.

Obeying the sense of life is a very important and practical matter in the Christian life. Everyone who is learning to follow the Lord in life must pay attention to this matter.

BELIEVERS HAVING THE SENSE OF LIFE ONCE THEY ARE SAVED

If we want to obey the sense of life, we must know six things, which we all possess once we are saved.

The Light of Life

1. "He who has the Son has the life"; "The life was the light of men" (1 John 5:12; John 1:4).

When we receive the Son of God as our Savior, we have the Son of God, and we also have the life because this life is in the Son of God. This life is the light of men, so when we have life, we have the light of life that enlightens us from within. With this life we do not need to seek outward light because we have a marvelous light within us, which is the Lord as the glorious life.

2. "I am the light of the world; he who follows Me...shall have the light of life" (John 8:12).

The Lord said that those who follow Him would have the light of life, but what is the light of life? How can we experience the light of life? Light enlightens and enables us to see; without light we are in darkness and cannot see. The light of life is the Lord's life in us as light. Previously we did not have the Lord's life, so our inner being was dark. Now we have the Lord's life as our light, so our inner being is bright, and we can see what is right and what is wrong, what pleases God and what is against His will. We have an inner seeing, which is actually an inner sense, because the Lord's life is shining in us.

For example, when we were offended in the past, we would become so angry that we could not be placated unless we lost our temper. Since we did not have the Lord's life and our inner being was dark, we even felt happy about losing our temper. With the light of life now shining in us, we do not feel happy when we lose our temper; instead, we feel uncomfortable. We even feel as if we have lost the Lord, and it is difficult to pray. Some sisters used to throw tantrums in their homes. The more tantrums they threw, the better they felt. This proves that they were in darkness. When they throw a tantrum now, they immediately sense that things are not right. This sense is not because of an outward human rule or exhortation. It also is not related to an outward biblical teaching; rather, it is from the inward light of life. When the light of life is shining in us, we can inwardly sense what God condemns and what He justifies. Therefore, the light of life is the Lord's life in us as our light; it makes our inner being bright so that we can see.

The Law of God Written on Our Hearts

1. "I will impart My laws into their mind, and on their hearts I will inscribe them" (Heb. 8:10; see also 10:16).

In the Old Testament the law of God was written on tablets of stone outside of man. But in the New Testament God imparts His laws into us and writes them on our hearts. How can God's law be imparted into us and written on our hearts? We can illustrate this by considering a dead tree that we command to sprout new branches, grow green leaves, bear red blossoms, and produce beautiful fruit. These commands are outside of the tree. They are worthless because a dead tree no longer has the power of life to carry out the requirements of our commandments. If we cannot give it life inwardly, a dead tree cannot respond to any commandment. But if God comes and enlivens the tree by giving it life, it will gradually sprout new branches, grow green leaves, bear red blossoms, and produce beautiful fruit. The life that God puts into a tree has a law for sprouting branches, growing leaves, bearing flowers, and producing fruit. When God puts life into something, He simultaneously includes everything related to this life. It can be said that God puts these laws into the tree and writes them on its heart.

On Mount Sinai God commanded man not to commit adultery, steal, or lie. These laws were outside of man. Now God has put His laws into us through His life, writing them on our hearts. His life includes His laws. When He puts His life into us, He also puts the laws of His life into us. When we have His life in us, we also have the laws of His life. Therefore, the laws that He writes in us are the law of life. The law of life within us spontaneously prevents us from committing adultery, stealing, lying, or doing things that are not pleasing to Him. God does not need to command us outwardly because the laws in His life cause us to know Him and His ordinances inwardly.

The Law of the Spirit of Life

1. "The law of the Spirit of life has freed me in Christ Jesus from the law of sin and of death" (Rom. 8:2).

This verse speaks of a law called the law of the Spirit of life. What is the law of the Spirit of life? It is a spontaneous power, a spontaneous function. When I wave my hand in front of a person's eyes, he spontaneously blinks. When I eat a meal, my stomach and intestines spontaneously digest the food. These are laws involving spontaneous powers and functions; they do not require an effort of our will or our strength to activate them. The law of the Spirit of life is also a spontaneous power and function that comes from the Spirit of life.

The Spirit of life is God's Spirit in our spirit. Since this Spirit is of life, His law must also be of life. Therefore, the law of the Spirit of life is also a law of life. A law does not necessarily have life, but life always has a law with a spontaneous power and function. Whether animal or vegetable, all life has a law and a spontaneous power and function. For example, flying is included in the law of the life of a bird; it is a spontaneous power of life in birds. Bearing fruit is included in the law of the life of a fruit tree; it is a spontaneous power of life in fruit trees. The higher that a life is, the stronger is its law and the greater is its spontaneous power and function. Since we have inwardly received the highest life from the Holy Spirit, it is the highest law, and it has the highest spontaneous power and function. This law, this spontaneous power and function, operates in us through God's Spirit to free us from the law of sin and of death, that is, from everything that is opposed to God. We do not need to make a determination to do something nor do we need to struggle and strive; the law of the Spirit of life operates in us spontaneously to manifest its power and function.

Since the law of the Spirit of life is also a law of life, it is one with the laws written on our hearts. A law that can be written on our hearts is related to life and emphasizes the function of life. Since this law is also the law of the Spirit of life, this law of life comes from the Holy Spirit in our spirit and emphasizes the function of the Holy Spirit.

God Operating in Us

1. "It is God who operates in you both the willing and the working for His good pleasure" (Phil. 2:13).

God is operating in us. This is a marvelous thing! We may know that God is in us, but we may not realize that God is operating in us. God is not in us apart from His work and activity. He is working and constantly operating in us. Regardless of our inward will or outward actions, He is always operating in us, causing us to know and obey His will for the accomplishment of His good pleasure.

2. "Now the God of peace...perfect you in every good work for the doing of His will, doing in us that which is well pleasing in His sight through Jesus Christ" (Heb. 13:20-21).

God is operating in us, doing that which is well pleasing in His sight through Jesus Christ, causing us to carry out His will. Therefore, His operation in us causes us to know His will and to realize what is well pleasing to Him.

Christ Living in Us

1. "Christ...lives in me" (Gal. 2:20).

Christ being in us is not only for Him to be our life but also for Him to live in us. His living in us means that He is working in us.

2. "Christ is in you"; "Jesus Christ is in you" (Rom. 8:10; 2 Cor. 13:5).

Christ is in us from the moment that we believe. Since we have faith in Christ, Christ is in us and He is living and working. He is not inactive in us.

The Teaching of the Anointing

1. "The anointing which you have received from Him abides in you, and you have no need that anyone teach you; but as His anointing teaches you concerning all things" (1 John 2:27).

The term *anointing* refers to the moving of the ointment, and in the Bible ointment refers to the Holy Spirit (Luke 4:18; Acts 10:38). Therefore, the anointing is the operation of the Holy Spirit. The Holy Spirit operates in us like the moving of ointment, anointing the Lord's will into our understanding. Thus, the anointing within teaches us concerning all things. Our knowledge of the Lord's requirements, of His leading, of what we should do before Him, and of how we should do it is taught by the moving of the ointment in us. Some brothers sense that the Lord wants them to deal with a certain matter; other brothers sense that the Lord wants them to offer up certain things. Some sisters sense that the Lord is touching their clothing and make-up; other sisters sense that the Lord is sending them to visit certain ones. These senses are anointed into them by the teaching of the anointing, which causes them to know the Lord's will and the Lord's desire. The teaching of the anointing within is very practical and precise.

The preceding six items all refer to matters related to God's life within us, and they speak of how God lives in us according to His life. These six items are connected. They are in accord with each other and are one. The Holy Spirit within us is Christ within us; Christ within us is God within us. The Triune God is living and operating in us to anoint His will into us; He does this through the enlightening of His life, which causes us to know Him and His will and to live in Him and in His will.

THE SENSE OF LIFE

When the Light of Life Shines within Us, We Have an Inward Sense, and What We Sense within Is Our Inward Seeing

Since the light of life is the enlightening of the Lord's life within us, this enlightening causes us to have an inward sense of life. What this life causes us to sense is what the light of life causes us to see. Our sense that a certain matter does not please the Lord is also our inward seeing that this matter does not please the Lord. Therefore, our inward sense is our inward seeing.

When the Law of God,
the Law of the Spirit of Life, Functions within Us,
It Gives Us an Inward Sense

God's law, which has been written on our hearts, and the law of the Spirit of life within us are both spontaneous functions of the Lord's life within us. When they function, we have an inward sense. This sense is the sense of life that gives us a feeling according to the function of the law of life. It is important to note that we often do not have much sensation when we follow the sense of life; however, when we go against this sense, we have a very clear feeling. When the digestion in our stomach is normal, we do not have much sense of it, but when something upsets our stomach, we have a strong feeling. When we disobey God, we disobey the sense of life in our actions, and the sense of life within us becomes especially strong. When we come to the meetings, we are following the sense of life, so we may not have much feeling related to it. However, when we go to a theater, we have a stronger feeling within because we are going against the sense of life.

The Operation of God with Us Also Gives Us
a Sense of Life

Because God's operation within us is a kind of action, it gives us an inward sense. If my hand touched someone's forehead, he would certainly feel it. When a person is very busy, he may not feel something touching him. But when he is quiet, he will feel the slightest touch or brush against him. When we are constantly busy, when we are disquieted, or when we are nervous and worried about many matters, we cannot sense God's operation within us. If we would be willing to quiet ourselves, God's operation within us would arise in our sensation, and we would feel God operating within us. With respect to God, His operation in us is a kind of work, and with respect to us, it produces a sense of life in us. If our condition is proper, we will feel a sense of life.

Christ in Us Is Not Only Alive but also Living, so We Have an Inward Sense of Him

Christ in us not only has life and is alive, but He also is living actively in us by His life. As He lives in us, He takes action, so He can be felt by us inwardly. Because this sense comes from the activity of His life within us, it must belong to life and should be considered as a sense of life.

Having an Inward Sense of the Teaching of the Anointing within Us because the Anointing of the Ointment Is the Speaking and the Shining of the Revelation of the Holy Spirit within Us

The ointment teaches us inwardly through its anointing. The teaching of the anointing is the Holy Spirit speaking within us; it is the inward light of the revelation of the Holy Spirit. All of these different terms refer to one thing, that is, the operation of the Holy Spirit within us. Since this operation is the moving of the Holy Spirit within our spirit, we certainly have a sense of life in our spirit. This sense of life gives us a feeling in our spirit, which means that it causes us to hear things from the Holy Spirit and see things through the Holy Spirit.

Therefore, we not only have life within us, but we also have the sense of life. Within us the light of life enlightens, the law of life manifests its function, God operates in us, Christ lives in us, and the Holy Spirit anoints us. These are all related to the sense of life which is rich and strong.

THE RESPONSIBILITY OF THE BELIEVERS TOWARD THE SENSE OF LIFE

Walking according to the Spirit— Setting the Mind on the Spirit

1. "Walk...according to the spirit...the mind set on the spirit" (Rom. 8:4-6).

Our inner sense of life comes from the Holy Spirit and is

in our spirit. Thus, our first responsibility with regard to the sense of life is to walk according to the spirit and to set our mind on the spirit in all things. To walk according to the spirit and to set our mind on the spirit are to walk according to the sense of life, to set our mind on the sense of life, and to obey the sense of life. With respect to the sense of life, the most important thing is obedience. Regardless of the matter, as soon as we have an inner sense of life related to it, we should obey the sense of life immediately. This is the most precious thing about being a Christian. If we want to obey the sense of life, we should walk according to the spirit and set the mind on the spirit.

Caring for the Sense of Life and Peace

1. "The mind set on the spirit is life and peace" (Rom. 8:6).

The sense of life in us is also a sense of peace. When we obey it, it gives us a feeling not only of life but also of peace. Therefore, regardless of the situation, as soon as we feel death instead of life and feel unease instead of peace, we should immediately stop what we are doing. We must always care for the sense of life and peace. If we would care for life and peace in this way, we must set our mind on the spirit. Only by setting the mind on the spirit can there be life and peace.

2. "Go in peace" (Luke 7:50).

In Luke 7, after a woman was saved, the Lord told her to go in peace. The Lord's word indicates that after we are saved, we receive peace. This peace is within us and causes us to have an inward sense. Whenever we want to do something that pleases God, we sense peace inwardly; otherwise, we do not have peace. When we do what is in agreement with the sense of peace, we have peace. When we do what is not in agreement with the sense of peace, we do not have peace. After we are saved, we should go the way of peace. After being saved, our living should be a living of peace. We should go in peace, and we should live in peace. Often we do not have the sense of peace in our walk and living even though we say that we are at peace. Just saying that we are at peace does not mean that we are at peace. In every single matter, we must be inwardly at peace. Sometimes brothers and sisters say that they have an inward peace, but their peace is not spontaneous but rather the product of their rationalization. Some brothers want to do something even though they have no inward peace. Consequently, they convince themselves that they have peace. Peace that comes from this kind of rationalization is not spontaneous. It is a peace that comes from reasoning, not a peace that comes spontaneously. As soon as they stop their reasoning, they are not peaceful. We should not be like this. We must allow the sense of peace to work spontaneously in us.

3. "Who, being past feeling,...but you did not so learn Christ" (Eph. 4:19-20).

The Gentiles have cast away all feeling. They commit sins and do evil without caring for their inner consciousness. But we, having learned Christ, should not be like this. We need to care for the feeling within us. The Gentiles have a conscience that is defiled and on the brink of death; they are darkened in their understanding. The feelings within us, however, are strong. The precious blood has cleansed our conscience, and because we are regenerated, our conscience has been revived. It is fresh and keen. The understanding in our mind has been renewed and is bright and proper. Our spirit has been made alive and has spiritual intuition. Moreover, we have the life of God and the Spirit of God in our spirit strengthening the feelings within us that are of life and consistent with light. Therefore, we have a living, keen, rich, proper, strong, and powerful feeling that enables us to sense whether or not any matter is pleasing to God. As followers of Christ, we should absolutely obey and care for this feeling. We should do what this feeling approves of and wants us to do, and we should refrain from doing whatever it disagrees with and prohibits us from doing.

Obeying with Fear and Trembling

1. "Obeyed...with fear and trembling; for it is God who operates in you both the willing and the working" (Phil. 2:12-13).

When we sense God's operation in us, whether it is His

willing or His working, we should obey with fear and trembling. Fear is our inward feeling, and trembling is our outward attitude. We should obey because we are afraid of disobeying God, who is operating in us. When we obey the inward sense, we obey God. We should be absolute and obey with fear and trembling.

Fellowshipping with the Lord according to the Teaching of the Anointing

1. "As His anointing teaches you...abide in Him" (1 John 2:27).

The teaching of the anointing causes us to know the Lord and His life. Therefore, we should abide in the Lord and fellowship with Him according to this teaching. To be according to the teaching of the anointing is to obey the moving of the Holy Spirit within us. This is the only way for us to be in the Lord and to have the fellowship of life with the Lord.

THE MAINTENANCE, RECOVERY, AND INCREASE OF THE SENSE OF LIFE

In order for a believer not to lose the sense of life, he must be in fear and trembling as he cares for and obeys every inward feeling of life. Only this will maintain the sense of life within.

The sense of life within a believer becomes dull when he ignores or disobeys it. If a believer begins to obey the small, flickering sense within, the sense of life will revive and recover. Although our sense of life sometimes becomes dull because we ignore or disobey it, it never dies out entirely or disappears completely. Something always remains. If we are willing to care for and obey even our small sense of life, we will immediately recover. In order to recover the sense of life, we must care for and obey it.

The sense of life within a believer becomes keen when he obeys it. If a believer continues to obey everything that he feels, his sense of life will become even stronger and keener. The more a believer obeys the sense of life, the more the sense of life increases. Therefore, our obedience increases the sense of life within us.

THE RESULT OF THE BELIEVERS' OBEYING THE SENSE OF LIFE

Sensing Life and Peace

1. **"The mind set on the spirit is life and peace"** (Rom. 8:6).

To set the mind on the spirit is to obey the sense of life, and the result is life and peace. Life is satisfaction, and peace is rest. If we set our mind on the spirit and obey the sense of life, we will inwardly feel satisfaction and rest, and we will feel contented and peaceful. Otherwise, we will feel dissatisfied, as if we were missing something. We will feel restless and bothered, as if there were some problem. Obeying the sense of life is the only way for our life to be nourished and for our hearts and spirits to obtain rest. This is true even in the matters of preaching the Word and prayer. We must set the mind on the spirit to be able to touch the Lord's presence, that is, to touch life and peace. When we obey the sense of life, the more we preach, the more we feel satisfied and receive the inward supply. The more we pray, the more we are at peace and feel watered in spirit. This sense of satisfaction and rest is the result of obeying the sense of life.

Abiding in the Lord

1. **"As His anointing teaches you...abide in Him"** (1 John 2:27).

If we walk according to the teaching of the anointing, we will abide in the Lord. To abide in the Lord means that we are not separated from Him and have constant fellowship with Him. If we desire this, we must act according to the anointing within, and we must obey the sense of life from the Holy Spirit. When we live in the anointing and obey the sense of life in our actions, we are kept in our fellowship with the Lord and we can constantly abide in Him. Abiding in the Lord is a result of obeying the sense of life.

Working Out Our Salvation

1. **"Work out your own salvation with fear and trembling"** (Phil. 2:12).

We have received salvation, but after receiving salvation, we must work or live it out. If we want to live out our salvation, we must obey God, who is operating in us, with fear and trembling; that is, we must obey the sense of life that comes from God's operation within us. If we are willing to obey, we will live out God's salvation.

God's salvation is God Himself. Therefore, for us to live out God's salvation is to live out God Himself. Hence, in order for us to live out His salvation, He personally operates in us, causing us to live Him out. His operating in us gives us a sense of life and gives us feelings through this sense of life. Therefore, when we obey the sense of life, we obey God's operation in us and we obey God. As we obey Him in this way, we spontaneously live Him out. Our living Him out is our living, our working out, of His salvation. Working out God's salvation is another result of obeying the sense of life.

Accomplishing the Good Pleasure of God

1. "It is God who operates in you both the willing and the working for His good pleasure" (Phil. 2:13).

God operates in us to accomplish His good pleasure. Therefore, when we obey His operating, that is, when we obey the sense of life, we can accomplish His good pleasure.

2. "God...for the doing of His will, doing in us that which is well pleasing in His sight" (Heb. 13:20-21).

God causes us to do His will, doing in us that which is well pleasing in His sight not merely through outward Bible teaching or environmental leading but even more through operating within us to let us know His will and to give us the strength to do that which is well pleasing to Him. We sense His will and His good pleasure through the sense of life given to us by His operation. When we obey the sense of life, we spontaneously obey the will of God and do that which is well pleasing to Him. Therefore, obeying the will of God and accomplishing His good pleasure are also certain results of obeying the sense of life.

We need to see the importance of obeying the sense of life. The supply of life and our growth in life, our intimacy with the Lord and fellowship with Him, the working out of our

salvation and our expression of Him, our obedience to His
will, and the accomplishment of His good pleasure all hinge
on our obeying the sense of life. Every spiritual matter
between God and us is entered into properly and carried out
through this one matter—obeying the sense of life.

CHAPTER TWENTY-TWO

LIVING IN THE FELLOWSHIP OF LIFE

I. The fellowship of life.

II. The two aspects of the fellowship of life:
   A. Fellowship with the apostles and the church that they represent.
   B. Fellowship with God and the Lord Jesus.

III. The means of the fellowship of life:
   A. The Holy Spirit.

IV. Another way of speaking of the fellowship of life:
   A. Abiding in the Lord.

V. The believers' responsibilities toward the fellowship of life:
   A. Continuing steadfastly.
   B. Obeying the teaching of the anointing.
   C. Walking in the light.
   D. Confessing our sins.

VI. The results of the fellowship of life:
   A. Obtaining the light of God.
   B. Obtaining the cleansing of the blood.
   C. Having the Lord abiding in us.
   D. Bearing much fruit to glorify God.
   E. Having our prayers accomplished.

VII. Breaking the fellowship of life:
   A. The life relationship between the believers and God never being able to be broken.
   B. The life fellowship between the believers and God being able to be broken.

VIII. The recovery of the fellowship of life:
   A. By confessing our sins.

IX. The relationship between the sense of life and the fellowship of life.

X. The danger to the believers of not living in the fellowship of life:

    A. Losing the function of life and suffering loss.

    B. Being fearful and ashamed.

Living in the fellowship of life, like obeying the sense of life, is a very important and practical matter in the Christian life. All those who pursue growth in the spiritual life must pay attention to this matter.

THE FELLOWSHIP OF LIFE

1. "We...report to you the eternal life...that you also may have fellowship with us, and indeed our fellowship is with the Father and with His Son Jesus Christ" (1 John 1:2-3).

Two things are particularly spoken of in this verse: eternal life and fellowship. The eternal life is the life of God. This life causes us to have fellowship. Therefore, the fellowship that we have comes out of the life of God. Since both the nature and content of this fellowship belong to God's life, it is called the fellowship of life.

The fellowship of life involves the life of God entering into us and causing us to have a life-flow with God, the Lord, and all those who have the life of God. In it we can share our innermost feelings and are mingled into one with God, the Lord, and all those who have the life of God.

Every kind of life has fellowship and requires fellowship. The higher a life is, the greater is its capacity to fellowship and the deeper is its need for fellowship. The life of God is the highest life, so it has the greatest capacity to fellowship and the deepest need for fellowship. This life is in us, enabling us to have the highest fellowship and giving us a very deep need for this highest fellowship.

THE TWO ASPECTS
OF THE FELLOWSHIP OF LIFE

Fellowship with the Apostles
and the Church That They Represent

1. "We...report to you the eternal life...that you also may have fellowship with us" (1 John 1:2-3).

The fellowship of life that comes into us has two aspects: one is fellowship with those who have the life of God and the other is fellowship with God and the Lord. The apostle John says that they report the eternal life so that we may have fellowship with them. *We* refers to the apostles. The apostles represent the church (1 Cor. 12:28). The church is composed of all who have God's life. Therefore, the life of God causes us to have fellowship with the apostles, which is the same as causing us to have fellowship with the church, all who have the life of God.

When the life of God comes into us, it spontaneously causes us to have fellowship with those who have the life of God. We become one with them in life because this fellowship is in the one life of God. Although many have this life, the life is one. We have received the one life of God, so the life that we have is the same one life. In this one life we can be one and have fellowship with one another in oneness. This is similar to a light in a room and thousands of lights in a city being one in the one flow of electricity. When we meet a brother or sister in the Lord, there is an inward response and fellowship if there are no barriers in us. It is as if there is a flow of electricity between us. This kind of fellowship is very precious. It gives us the watering and the supply of life.

The life of God not only causes us to fellowship with the children of God but also requires us to do so. If we have fellowship in God's life with the children of God, we feel inwardly satisfied, comfortable, proper, and natural. If we do not have this fellowship, we feel depressed, miserable, and unfulfilled. This proves that the life of God requires us to fellowship with the children of God. If we respond to the requirement of God's life in us, we will live in God's life; that is, we will live in the fellowship of God's life.

2. "Those then who received his word were baptized...They continued steadfastly in the teaching and the fellowship of the apostles" (Acts 2:41-42).

At the time of Pentecost everyone who heard and believed continued in the fellowship of the apostles after being baptized. This means that they continuously had fellowship in God's life with all the believers. This fellowship is called the fellowship of the apostles because the Lord's life is imparted to people through the reporting of the apostles, which makes them the church, the Lord's Body. The apostles also represent the church produced by the Lord's life. Thus, the fellowship of the apostles is the fellowship of the church. If a person has fellowship with the apostles, as in 1 John 1, he has fellowship with the church. This fellowship in the believers is from the Lord's life. They share a common fellowship in the one life of the Lord and should continue to have fellowship in the unchanging life of the Lord. When we fellowship with the believers in this way, we continue in the fellowship of the apostles.

Fellowship with God and the Lord Jesus

1. **"That you also may have fellowship with us, and indeed our fellowship is with the Father and with His Son Jesus Christ"** (1 John 1:3).

The apostles' fellowship is with God and with the Lord Jesus. Therefore, the fellowship of the church that they represent is also the fellowship of God and the fellowship of the Lord. If we are in the fellowship of the apostles and in the fellowship of the church that they represent, we are also in the fellowship of God and the Lord. Conversely, if we are in the fellowship of God and the Lord, we must also be in the fellowship of the apostles and the church, because the fellowship of the Lord and the fellowship of the church are two aspects of the same fellowship. They are actually just one fellowship.

On the one hand, the life of the Lord causes us to have fellowship with God and with the Lord, and on the other hand, it causes us to have fellowship with the church represented by the apostles and with all those who have the Lord's life. This is similar to electricity in the light in a room. On the one hand, the electricity causes the light to have fellowship with the electric power plant, and on the other hand, it causes the light in the room to have fellowship with all the lights in the city. If the light breaks its fellowship with the electric power plant, its fellowship with the other lights in the city is also broken. In the same way, if a person with the Lord's life breaks his fellowship with the Lord, his fellowship with those who have the Lord's life is also broken. Even though two believers have the Lord's life, they will not have the fellowship of life if either breaks his fellowship with the Lord. If a believer has a problem with the Lord, it will be apparent to others because they will not be able to fellowship with him since he is not connected to the electric power plant—the Lord. Thus, the two cannot connect.

If we are living in fellowship with the Lord, when we touch another person who is in fellowship with the Lord, there is an immediate inward life reaction. This is the fellowship of life. This is similar to when a magnet touches a piece of metal—there is an immediate reaction. A missionary from Norway once came to Shantung to preach the gospel. Her topic was always regeneration. When she finished the message, she would immediately hurry to the door of the hall and ask each person as they went out whether they had been regenerated. It did not matter whether they were pastors, elders, or preachers; she asked everyone the same question. Once she asked a preacher named Mr. Wang, who later became a very good brother, whether he had been regenerated. When he said, "Yes," she said that his voice did not sound as if he had been regenerated. When he heard this, he was very angry. After he went home, the Holy Spirit worked in his heart, and after a couple of days he thoroughly repented, confessed his sins with tears, and received the Lord as his Savior. As soon as he finished praying, he hurried to the missionary's house. Before he could say anything, she said, "Thank the Lord, you have been saved." The fellowship of the Lord's life within us is very marvelous and spiritual. It causes us to have fellowship both with God and the Lord and with those who have the Lord's life. We have the Lord's life in us, and this life causes us to have fellowship with the Lord and to have fellowship with one another. The fellowship that we have with others is the fellowship that we have with the Lord, because these two aspects of fellowship are in the one fellowship of life.

THE MEANS OF THE FELLOWSHIP OF LIFE

The Holy Spirit

1. "The fellowship of the Holy Spirit" (2 Cor. 13:14).

The Lord's life is in the Holy Spirit. It comes into us and is in us through the Holy Spirit. Our fellowship in the Lord's life is through the Holy Spirit; therefore, it is also called the fellowship of the Holy Spirit. Whether we fellowship with

God and with the Lord or with the church or with a saint, all of our fellowship is in the Holy Spirit and through the Holy Spirit. The fellowship of life, which is in and through the Holy Spirit, becomes our life experience and spiritual reality only when we live in the Holy Spirit and follow the Holy Spirit.

2. "If any fellowship of spirit" (Phil. 2:1).

Since the fellowship of life is in and through the Holy Spirit, it comes out of the Holy Spirit's operation in us. The Holy Spirit operates in us and causes us, even requiring and compelling us, to have fellowship with the Lord and with the saints in His life. If we follow and mind the Spirit, He will lead us to live in the fellowship of the Lord's life.

ANOTHER WAY OF SPEAKING OF THE FELLOWSHIP OF LIFE

Abiding in the Lord

1. "Even as it has taught you, abide in Him" (1 John 2:27).

Our relationship with the Lord is so close that we can abide in the Lord. To abide in the Lord means to not have any barriers between the Lord and us, which is just to fellowship with the Lord. Therefore, abiding in the Lord is another way of speaking of our fellowship in the Lord's life. When we fellowship with the Lord in His life, we abide in Him, just as a light abides in the power plant by abiding in the fellowship with the power plant.

2. "Abide in Me and I in you. As the branch cannot bear fruit of itself unless it abides in the vine, so neither can you unless you abide in Me. I am the vine; you are the branches. He who abides in Me and I in him, he bears much fruit; for apart from Me you can do nothing" (John 15:4-5).

After reading these verses we should understand what it means to abide in the Lord. The branches of the vine have fellowship with the vine. This is their abiding in the vine. The Lord is the vine; we are the branches. Our living in the Lord and our fellowship with Him are like branches abiding in the vine.

To be in the Lord and to abide in the Lord are different. To be in the Lord is a matter of salvation; to abide in the Lord is a matter of fellowship. As soon as we are saved, we are in the Lord, but we must abide in the Lord to fellowship with Him. Although some are in the Lord, they do not abide in Him. We must not have any barriers between the Lord and us, and we must have fellowship to abide in the Lord. Therefore, all who are saved and in the Lord should fellowship with the Lord and abide in Him.

THE BELIEVERS' RESPONSIBILITIES TOWARD THE FELLOWSHIP OF LIFE

Continuing Steadfastly

1. "They continued steadfastly in...the fellowship" (Acts 2:42).

As soon as we receive the Lord's life, we enter into the fellowship of His life. Henceforth, we should continue to live in the fellowship of life. We are responsible for not breaking the fellowship of life.

Obeying the Teaching of the Anointing

1. "Even as it has taught you, abide in Him" (1 John 2:27).

If we want to continue in the fellowship of the Lord's life, we must abide in the Lord, according to the teaching of the anointing. We must obey the teaching of the anointing. In the previous chapter, we saw that the teaching of the anointing is the operation of the Holy Spirit in us. We must obey the Holy Spirit's operation in us and abide in the Lord according to this operation. In this way we can live in the fellowship of the Lord's life without interruption. As soon as we disobey the operation of the Holy Spirit, however, our fellowship with the Lord will be broken.

Walking in the Light

1. "If we walk in the light as He is in the light, we have fellowship with one another" (1 John 1:7).

The fellowship of life brings us into the Lord's light and requires us to live and walk in the Lord's light. We must live and walk in the Lord's light in order to maintain the fellowship of life with the Lord and the saints. As soon as we stop living in the light of the Lord, we lose the ability to fellowship with the Lord, and we will not be able to fellowship with His people in His life.

Confessing Our Sins

1. "If we walk in the light...we have fellowship with one another, and the blood of Jesus His Son cleanses us from every sin...If we confess our sins, He is faithful and righteous to forgive us our sins and cleanse us" (1 John 1:7, 9).

If we live in the fellowship of the Lord's life, we are indeed in the light of life. This light of life causes us to see our sins. Once we see our sins, that is, once we are conscious of them in the fellowship of the light of life, we must confess our sins to God. If we are willing to confess our sins to God, we will be forgiven and cleansed by God. We will then be brought more deeply into the fellowship of the Lord's life. If we do not confess our sins, they will remain with us and cause our fellowship with the Lord to be broken.

THE RESULTS OF THE FELLOWSHIP OF LIFE

Obtaining the Light of God

1. "God is light...If we say that we have fellowship with Him and yet walk in the darkness, we lie...But if we walk in the light as He is in the light, we have fellowship with one another" (1 John 1:5-7).

God is light. If we fellowship with Him, we will have His light. Therefore, the fellowship of life brings us into the light of God so that we may have His light. Being in darkness is proof that we do not have fellowship with God or that our fellowship has been broken. If we have fellowship with God or with His children, we certainly are in the light of God. The fellowship of life and the light of God cannot be separated. If we are in the fellowship of life, we are in the light of God. If we are not in the light of God, we have lost the fellowship of life.

Obtaining the Cleansing of the Blood

1. "If we walk in the light as He is in the light, we

have fellowship with one another, and the blood of Jesus His Son cleanses us from every sin" (1 John 1:7).

In the fellowship of life, if we are enlightened by the Lord's light to see our sins and then confess them to God, the blood of the Lord cleanses us from our sins. Therefore, after we are saved, we can be cleansed from sin by the blood of the Lord in the fellowship of the Lord's life. If our confession lacks the conviction that comes from the Lord's light, we will not receive the cleansing of the Lord's blood. If we want to receive the cleansing of the Lord's blood, we must be enlightened by the Lord's light of life in the fellowship of the Lord's life. The cleansing of the Lord's blood is not separate from the fellowship of the Lord's life. If we do not have the fellowship of the Lord's life, we cannot be enlightened by the Lord's light of life. If we are not enlightened by the Lord's light of life, we cannot see our sins to confess them to God. If our sins are not seen and confessed, we cannot be cleansed by the Lord's blood. If we sin after we are saved, those sins must be confessed to God in order for us to be cleansed by the Lord's blood. To confess to God we must be enlightened, and to be enlightened we must live in the fellowship of life. Therefore, the sins that we commit after we are saved are cleansed away by the Lord's blood through the fellowship of life.

Having the Lord Abiding in Us

1. "He who abides in Me and I in him" (John 15:5, see also v. 4).

If we live in the fellowship of the Lord's life, we abide in the Lord, and when we abide in the Lord, we have the Lord abiding in us. When the Lord abides in us, He becomes our life, power, joy, and peace so that we may enjoy Him and all the riches of His life in our practical experience. Therefore, the Lord's abiding in us to be our all is also a result of living in the fellowship of life.

Bearing Much Fruit to Glorify God

1. "He who abides in Me and I in him, he bears much fruit" (John 15:5, see also v. 4).

When a branch abides in the vine without any barriers

between itself and the vine, it receives a rich supply of sap and bears much fruit. Similarly, when we abide in the Lord and fellowship with Him, we receive the supply of His life and bear much fruit. Therefore, the fruit in our spiritual life issues from our abiding in the Lord and fellowshipping with Him.

2. "In this is My Father glorified, that you bear much fruit" (John 15:8).

When we bear much spiritual fruit, God is glorified because His life is expressed. If we want to bear much spiritual fruit, we must abide in the Lord and fellowship with Him. Bearing much spiritual fruit to glorify God and to express His life is a result of the fellowship of life.

Having Our Prayers Accomplished

1. "If you abide in Me and My words abide in you, ask whatever you will, and it shall be done for you" (John 15:7).

According to the Lord's promise, if we abide in Him and His words abide in us, whatever we ask will be done for us. This shows that abiding in the Lord and fellowshipping with Him are prerequisites for the matters we pray about to come to pass. Having our prayers accomplished is a result of abiding in the Lord and fellowshipping with Him. If we want our prayers to be accomplished, we must abide in the Lord and fellowship with Him. When we abide in Him, we know His heart's desire and purpose and can pray according to His heart's desire and purpose. Since our asking will be according to the Lord's heart's desire and one with His purpose, the Lord will accomplish it. We must abide in the Lord and fellowship with Him in order for our prayer to be one with the Lord's purpose.

BREAKING THE FELLOWSHIP OF LIFE

The Life Relationship between the Believers and God Never Being Able to Be Broken

1. "They shall by no means perish forever...And no one can snatch them out of My Father's hand" (John 10:28-29).

Our life relationship with God can never be broken because we have received the eternal life of God that enables us to by no means perish forever. Furthermore, God's hand is powerful; nothing can snatch us out of His hand. Whether we speak from the aspect of God's eternal life or from the aspect of God's powerful hand, the result is that our life relationship with God can never be broken.

The Life Fellowship between the Believers and God Being Able to Be Broken

1. "If we walk in the light as He is in the light, we have fellowship with one another" (1 John 1:7).

Our fellowship of life with God is based on our life relationship with God. This life relationship cannot be broken, but the fellowship of life can be and is broken very easily because of our sins and disobedience. The life relationship between a child and his mother can never be broken, but it is very easy for their fellowship to be broken. When a child does something wrong, he does not want to see his mother. For example, a mother may say to her child, "I am going out for a while. Do not eat any candy while I am away." But after she leaves, he may take some candy and eat it. Normally, when he obeys his mother, he is happy to see her, but when his mother returns, he will run away from her if he has eaten some candy. When she comes into the living room, he will run into the kitchen, and when she comes into the kitchen, he will run into the living room. An experienced mother will realize that he has eaten some candy.

If we walk in the Lord's light, we are living in the fellowship of the Lord's life. However, we often fail to live in the Lord's light. Often we are disobedient and sin; therefore, we lose the fellowship of the Lord's life. As soon as we stop living in the Lord's light, being disobedient or sinful, our fellowship in the Lord's life is broken. We will not be able to fellowship with the Lord, and we will not want to fellowship with the brothers and sisters. Nevertheless, this does not mean that our life relationship with the Lord has been broken. It can never be broken. Nothing can break our life relationship with the Lord. However, even a small problem with God, a little argument with God, a small amount of disobedience, or a tiny sin can break our fellowship in the Lord's life.

THE RECOVERY OF THE FELLOWSHIP OF LIFE

By Confessing Our Sins

1. "If we confess our sins, He is faithful and righteous to forgive us our sins and cleanse us from all unrighteousness" (1 John 1:9, see also v. 7).

Thank God! Although our life fellowship with Him can be broken, it can also be recovered. Since it is broken by our sin, it must be recovered through confessing our sins. If we are willing to confess our sins to God according to the Lord's enlightening, He is faithful and righteous according to His Word to forgive and cleanse us from our sins because of the Lord's blood. Thus, our fellowship with Him in life can be recovered. As soon as we confess our sins to God, He immediately forgives and cleanses us so that our conscience has peace and does not condemn us. Thus, our fellowship in life with Him is recovered. As soon as the child tells his mother that he is sorry for taking some candy, she will forgive him, and his fellowship with his mother will be recovered. We can recover our broken fellowship with God at any time. This recovery is based on the eternal efficacy of the Lord's precious blood, and it is accomplished through the confession of our sins.

THE RELATIONSHIP BETWEEN THE SENSE OF LIFE AND THE FELLOWSHIP OF LIFE

Once a believer neglects the sense of life, he immediately loses the fellowship of life. The fellowship of life is maintained in the sense of life, so once we neglect the sense of life, the fellowship of life is broken and lost.

Once a believer loses the fellowship of life, the sense of life is dulled. The fellowship of life is maintained through the sense of life, and the sense of life is sharpened by the fellowship of life. Thus, once the fellowship of life is lost, the sense of life is dulled.

Once a believer obeys even a fading sense of life, the fellowship of life is recovered. We lose the fellowship of life because we do not obey the sense of life. Therefore, if we obey even a fading sense of life, we will immediately recover the fellowship of life.

Once a believer recovers the fellowship of life, the sense of life becomes keener. The sense of life becomes dull when we lose the fellowship of life, but when we recover the fellowship of life, the sense of life is sharpened spontaneously.

The keener the sense of life is in a believer, the deeper is his fellowship. The deeper the fellowship of life is, the keener the sense of life is. These two are mutually related, forming a continuous cycle that causes the believers to grow in life. The sense of life depends upon the fellowship of life; the fellowship of life increases the sense of life. The more we have the sense of life, the more we have the fellowship of life, and the more we have the fellowship of life, the more we have the sense of life. As these two move in an ever-increasing cycle, the Lord's life within us grows.

THE DANGER TO THE BELIEVERS OF NOT LIVING IN THE FELLOWSHIP OF LIFE

Losing the Function of Life and Suffering Loss

1. "If one does not abide in Me, he is cast out as a branch and is dried up; and they gather them and cast them into the fire, and they are burned" (John 15:6).

The Lord said that if a saved one does not abide in Him—does not live in the fellowship of His life—"he is cast out as a branch and is dried up; and they gather them and cast them into the fire, and they are burned." The function of a branch is to bear fruit. In order for a branch to bear fruit, it must abide in the vine. Otherwise, it will lose the fruit-bearing function and suffer loss. If we do not abide in the Lord and fellowship with Him, it will be the same with us. However, this verse does not say that we will perish if we do not abide in the Lord. It says that we will lose the function of life and not be able to bear fruit to glorify God if we do not fellowship with the Lord. Thus, we will suffer loss. The Lord is not speaking of the requirements for salvation in this verse. He is speaking of the requirements for bearing fruit. If we do not fulfill these requirements, we will not lose our salvation. However, we will lose our ability to bear fruit and glorify God, so we will suffer loss (cf. 1 Cor. 3:15).

Being Fearful and Ashamed

1. "Abide in Him, so that if He is manifested, we may have boldness and not be put to shame from Him at His coming" (1 John 2:28).

If we abide in the Lord and fellowship with Him, we most certainly will walk before the Lord and live in His heart's desire. Thus, when He is manifested, we will have boldness and not be put to shame from Him. If we do not live like this, we will be afraid and ashamed when we see the Lord. This should be a warning for to us to live in the fellowship of the Lord.

CHAPTER TWENTY-THREE

CONSECRATION

I. The motive for consecration.

II. The significance of consecration:

    A. Following the will of God.

    B. Responding to the requirement of God's compassions.

    C. Allowing the Lord to enjoy His legal right.

    D. Expressing love for the Lord.

    E. God's testing of us.

    F. Testing and proving the Lord.

    G. Enjoying what the Lord has prepared.

    H. Gaining the Lord's blessing and supply.

    I. God's giving of grace.

III. What to consecrate:

    A. Ourselves.

    B. Our bodies.

    C. Everything.

IV. How to consecrate:

    A. Voluntarily.

    B. In secret.

V. The goal of consecration:

    A. To live to the Lord.

    B. To be a living sacrifice.

    C. To serve God.

    D. To follow the will of God.

    E. To let God work.

    F. To glorify God.

VI. The results of consecration:

    A. Understanding the will of God.

    B. Being able to be enlightened by the Lord.

C. Being able to have faith.
D. Being able to have spiritual experiences.
E. Enjoying all the riches of the Lord's glory.

Consecration is a great topic in the Bible.

THE MOTIVE FOR CONSECRATION

1. "The love of Christ constrains us because we have judged this, that One died for all, therefore all died; and He died for all that those who live may no longer live to themselves but to Him who died for them and has been raised" (2 Cor. 5:14-15).

Every consecrated believer is motivated by the Lord's love. We have a desire to consecrate ourselves because the Lord's love constrains us. We no longer live to ourselves but to the Lord because we have been constrained by the Lord's love. In the original Greek *constrain* means "to press." The Lord's love in our hearts becomes a great power pressing us to love the Lord and to live to Him. His love is like a rushing flood. We cannot help but consecrate ourselves to Him; we cannot withhold ourselves or what we have from Him.

Paul says that the Lord's love constrains us because we judge that the Lord died on our behalf. If we consider how the Lord died on our behalf, we would be constrained by His love. We should take time to consider how the Lord suffered for us, bore our sins, and tasted death on our behalf so that His love could constrain us. We should consider His love in His dying on our behalf, especially when we break bread to remember the Lord. The more we consider His love, the more our hearts will be touched and turned to Him. The Lord's love is the greatest love in the universe. Just as this love caused the Lord to die for us, it also causes us to live to Him.

2. "I exhort you therefore, brothers, through the compassions of God to present your bodies a living sacrifice" (Rom. 12:1).

Paul exhorted us through the compassions of God to consecrate ourselves. *Exhort* may also be rendered as "beg." The Holy Spirit within often begs us through the compassions of God, through God's love, to consecrate ourselves to God. The love of God is a great power used by the Holy Spirit to move us.

3. "Do you love Me more than these?...Do you love Me?...Follow Me" (John 21:15-22).

Peter was called by the Lord to follow Him, but he backslid and returned to his old profession of fishing. When the Lord came to seek him, He did not rebuke or blame Peter. He only asked, "Do you love Me more than these?" that is, more than his boats, his nets, the sea, the fish, the coals, and the loaves of bread. It is as if the Lord was quietly saying, "On the night that I was accused, you went to warm yourself, and you loved a charcoal fire to such an extent that you denied Me before those people. When I hid My visible presence from you, you went fishing to make a living and did not pay attention to My command. You warmed yourself but were put to shame. You went fishing to get something to eat but came up empty. Now I have prepared a charcoal fire, bread, and fish. You do not need to expend any energy; you do not need to do anything. If you want warmth, here is a charcoal fire. If you want to eat, here are bread and fish. But I want to ask, Do you love Me more than these—more than the charcoal fire, bread, and fish? Do you love Me? Follow Me!" The Lord's questioning in love touched and gained Peter. The Lord's love caused Peter to follow the Lord for his whole life until he was martyred for the Lord and glorified God by his death. (According to tradition, when Peter was arrested for the Lord's sake, he asked to be crucified upside down at the time of his death.)

In His love the Lord questions us in the same way. He often asks, "Do you love Me more than the world? Do you love Me more than your father, mother, wife (or husband), children, brothers, sisters, and friends? Do you love Me more than education, position, fame, family background, money, and life? Do you love Me?" Many have been truly conquered by the Lord's loving questioning and have become lovers of the Lord, pouring themselves and all that they have on the Lord for His gain. Oh, who can stand before the Lord's questioning in love? Who can resist the constraining of the Lord's love? When the Lord's love is revealed to us and works in us, we cannot escape. We can only consecrate ourselves and all that we have to the Lord. Once we are touched by His love, we must consecrate ourselves. This motivating power is not outside of us but inside of us. It burns like a raging fire that cannot be quenched.

THE SIGNIFICANCE OF CONSECRATION

Following the Will of God

1. "They gave themselves first to the Lord...through the will of God" (2 Cor. 8:5).

It is the will of God that the Lord would gain us. God called us and saved us so that we could be gained by the Lord. Therefore, when we consecrate ourselves to the Lord, we are following God's will. If we do not consecrate, we will obstruct the will that God purposed for the Lord. We will damage God's purpose for the Lord.

Responding to the Requirement of God's Compassions

1. "I exhort you...through the compassions of God to present your bodies" (Rom. 12:1).

Through His Spirit with His compassions, God's requirement in love for each of us is that we would present our bodies to Him. Consecration is a response to God's requirement.

Allowing the Lord to Enjoy His Legal Right

1. "Do you not know that...you are not your own? For you have been bought with a price. So then glorify God in your body" (1 Cor. 6:19-20).

The Lord not only saved us but also bought us. The Lord paid the price of His precious blood to buy us. Therefore, we are not our own; we are the Lord's. We do not have authority over ourselves. The authority over us is in the Lord's hands. Since we have been bought by the Lord, we should be completely His. Since the Lord bought us with His precious blood, He has the legal right to gain us. When we consecrate ourselves to the Lord and allow the Lord to gain us, we allow Him to enjoy His legal right. Without consecration, we are ungrateful with respect to His salvation and we are also negligent with respect to His legal rights over us.

2. "None of us lives to himself, and none dies to himself; for whether we live, we live to the Lord, and whether we die, we die to the Lord. Therefore whether we live or we die, we are the Lord's" (Rom. 14:7-8).

Since we are the Lord's, we should live to the Lord. We should not only live to the Lord but also die to the Lord. Whether we live or die, we should be to the Lord, not to ourselves. Consecration is needed in order for the Lord to gain us to this extent. Unconsecrated believers cannot glorify the Lord through their life or their death. Only those who are consecrated, who do not care about life or death, can glorify the Lord in their life or their death.

Expressing Love for the Lord

1. "Do you love Me?...Follow Me" (John 21:15-22).

Consecration comes out of loving the Lord. Therefore, consecration is the proper expression of love for the Lord, and it is also the highest expression of love for the Lord. The Lord told Peter that if he loved the Lord, he would follow Him. To follow the Lord is simply to give ourselves to the Lord. If we really love the Lord, we will consecrate ourselves to the Lord. The extent of our consecration is based on the depth of our love for the Lord.

God's Testing of Us

1. "God tested Abraham and said to him...Take now your son...and offer him there as a burnt offering" (Gen. 22:1-2).

God's desire for us to consecrate ourselves is a test of our love for God. Abraham loved God, so God asked him to offer his only son to Him. By doing this, God tested Abraham to see whether his love was absolute toward Him, whether Abraham loved Him more than everything else, even more than his only son.

2. "Proving also the genuineness of your love" (2 Cor. 8:8).

Proving is related to consecration—either in the consecration of our money or the consecration of ourselves. All consecration is a test—a proving—of our love toward the saints or toward God. It proves the level of our love.

Testing and Proving the Lord

1. "Bring the whole tithe to the storehouse...and

prove Me...whether I will open to you the windows of heaven and pour out blessing" (Mal. 3:10).

Consecration is God's testing and proving of us. It is also our testing and proving of God. God said to the children of Israel, "Bring the whole tithe to the storehouse"—to offer up what should be consecrated—"and prove Me, if you will... whether I will open to you the windows of heaven and pour out blessing." God meant that we could use our consecration to test Him, to prove how He will bless us because of our consecration. This was the case in Old Testament times but even more so in New Testament times. Throughout the ages many lovers of the Lord have tested and proven that God's blessing is practical and rich through their consecration. Many can testify of this from their experience. Oh, brothers and sisters, we can test God's riches by our consecration. God wants us to test Him and likes us to prove Him in this way.

Enjoying What the Lord Has Prepared

1. "Come, for all things are now ready" (Luke 14:17).

The Lord's grace has prepared everything for us. All things are ready. We need to come and enjoy. The way to enjoy what the Lord has prepared is not only by faith but also by consecration. Faith is for our initial participation, whereas consecration is for our practical enjoyment. An unconsecrated believer can only participate in what the Lord's grace has prepared. A consecrated believer can practically and experientially enjoy all that the Lord has prepared. All that the Lord's grace has prepared for us needs to be received and enjoyed through faith and consecration.

2. "Go...and offer him there as a burnt offering on one of the mountains of which I will tell you...On the mount of Jehovah it will be provided" (Gen. 22:2, 14).

Through his offering up of Isaac, Abraham enjoyed what God had prepared, and he experienced the reality of a particular name of God—*Jehovah-jireh,* which means "Jehovah will provide." Many like this name, but we must realize that the reality of this name is revealed on the mountain of consecration. If we do not go to the mountain of consecration, we cannot taste the sweetness of *Jehovah-jireh.* If we do not consecrate, we cannot enjoy what God has provided. When we offer our beloved "Isaac," our only "son," to God, we can meet and enjoy what God has provided for us in His precious name, which is just in Himself. When Hudson Taylor was first called, he visited the sick wife of a poor man. When the man begged him for help, he had only one coin in his pocket, which he was planning to use for food the next day. He thought, "In order to help this poor man, I have to give him the coin, but then I will not have anything to eat tomorrow. If only there was a way to give half of the coin's value to him while keeping the other half to buy food, but this is not possible." The man continued to beg for help, and at the same time the Holy Spirit spoke within him to give the coin to the poor man. Then he gave the man the coin. The next morning he received a packet containing a pair of gloves wrapped in a sheet of blank paper, and there was a coin in the gloves. The coin was worth four times as much as the one he had given to the poor man. Through this he enjoyed God's special provision; he later made *Jehovah-jireh* the motto for the China Inland Mission.

Gaining the Lord's Blessing and Supply

1. "Because you have done this thing and have not withheld your son, your only son, I will surely bless you and will greatly multiply your seed like the stars of the heavens and like the sand which is on the seashore" (Gen. 22:16-17).

Because Abraham offered up his only son, God blessed him greatly, multiplying his seed as the stars of the heavens and as the sand upon the seashore. Abraham offered up one son, and God gave him many descendants. Abraham's consecration to God caused him to gain something from God. If we want more blessing from God, we must consecrate what we have to God. Consecration brings in God's blessing. It is the way for us to gain God's blessing.

2. "Bring the whole tithe...I will open to you the windows of heaven and pour out blessing for you until there is no room for it" (Mal. 3:10).

God told the children of Israel that if they would bring

the whole tithe—consecrate—He would open the windows of heaven and pour out immeasurable blessings to them. Consecration can open the windows of heaven for us and bring down God's blessing.

3. "Honor Jehovah with your substance / And with the firstfruits of all your produce; / Then your barns will be filled with plenty, / And your vats will burst open with new wine" (Prov. 3:9-10).

If we honor God with our consecration, God will cause us to be "filled with plenty" and to "burst open" with blessings. A poor and lacking person is an unconsecrated person. Consecration will not make us poor nor will it cause us to decrease. Instead, it will give us plenty, even to the point of bursting open. If we want to be a person with plenty and bursting open, we must consecrate.

4. "We do not have anything here except five loaves and two fish. And He said, Bring them here to Me...And they all ate and were satisfied. And they took up what was left over of the broken pieces, twelve handbaskets full" (Matt. 14:17-18, 20).

When the Lord fed the five thousand, the disciples had only five loaves and two fish. If they had kept this food for themselves, there would not have been enough even for themselves. However, they brought the loaves and fish to the Lord. This brought in a great blessing in which the disciples and more than five thousand people ate and were satisfied. The leftovers were more than what they had originally offered. When we consecrate, putting ourselves and what we have into the Lord's hands, many are blessed. Our consecration can bring in and express the riches of the Lord's blessing. The Lord often expresses the riches of His blessing through our consecration.

5. "Give, and it will be given to you" (Luke 6:38).

The Lord said that if we give, it will be given to us. This can be illustrated by a water faucet. The more that water flows out, the more that water can flow in. If water does not flow out, nothing can flow in. If we want to gain, we must give. If we want to receive, we must give. Our giving is our receiving. Our consecration is the path to gaining the supply. Often we do not receive a supply because we have not consecrated or given anything out. Our economics are different from that of the world. We do not count how much we gain in order to see how much we can spend; we count how much we have given out to measure our gain. We must give before we can receive. We should not be like the Dead Sea, which has no outlet. We should be a channel of living water that flows without ceasing.

6. "He who bountifully supplies seed to the sower... will supply and multiply your seed" (2 Cor. 9:10).

According to the apostle's word in this verse, consecration is a sowing. The result of sowing is not loss but gain—multiplied gain. If we sow one seed, we will reap thirty, sixty, or even one hundredfold. Therefore, in order to gain we must first sow our seed. If we want to reap, we must sow. Only consecration can give us a rich harvest. A person who is not consecrated cannot see God's riches, but praise the Lord, a truly consecrated person cannot help but express God's riches. Although he is not as rich as many worldly people, he is always a channel of transmission flowing out God's riches and enriching many (6:10). This should be our condition. We should let everything flow out so that God's riches can flow in. We should sow everything to bring in the abundant harvest of God's riches. We should not save up, shut up, or withhold. We must flow out, sow, and consecrate. Consecration is always the way to bring in God's blessing. The more we consecrate, the more we bring in God's blessing. The degree of God's blessing depends on the degree of our consecration. When we withhold ourselves and what we have, we block the path for God's blessing. What we put forth and give up for the Lord, the gospel, the church, and sinners may seemingly empty our hands to the point of having nothing, but something great will flow in and out of us. This is true in regard to spiritual things even more than material things. Oh, the way of consecration not only brings in God's blessing but even more, God Himself! May we all take this way. May we all consecrate.

God's Giving of Grace

1. "We make known to you...the grace of God which

has been given in the churches of Macedonia, that...
the depth of their poverty abounded unto the riches of
their liberality" (2 Cor. 8:1-2).

We often think that consecration is giving something to
God, but according to the apostle's word, consecration is the
grace of God given to us. The liberality of the churches in
Macedonia was the grace of God that had been given to them.
God gives us grace within so that we can have a consecration
without. Because the grace of God operates and supplies us
within, we experience the act of consecration without. Thus,
the act of consecration is grace received from God.

WHAT TO CONSECRATE

Ourselves

1. "They gave themselves first to the Lord" (2 Cor.
8:5).

God wants us, not our money (12:14); therefore, the first
thing that we should consecrate to the Lord is ourselves. The
churches in Macedonia gave themselves first to the Lord and
then offered up everything that they had according to God's
will. We must offer up ourselves first; otherwise, our consecration has no value. In 1948 in Shanghai, a wealthy man
wanted to buy us a bus from America to use for the gospel.
However, we were concerned that he had not given himself to
the Lord, so we could not receive it. Christianity has misrep-
resented God in the matter of consecration, placing more
emphasis on money than on the person. This is a terrible
shame! It is not pleasing to the Lord. The Lord wants man,
not the things of man. We must first offer ourselves to the
Lord and let the Lord gain us before our things will be acceptable to Him.

**2. "Present yourselves to God as alive from the
dead"** (Rom. 6:13).

We must present our resurrected new man in Christ to the
Lord, not our old man. Our old man was crucified with Christ
and terminated. In Christ, we are those who are alive from
the dead. In our standing in resurrection, we should present
ourselves to God so that God can gain us in His resurrected
new creation.

Our Bodies

1. "Present your bodies a living sacrifice" (Rom. 12:1).

We are in our bodies. If we want to give ourselves to the Lord, we must present our bodies to Him. If we do not, our consecration is abstract and vague; it is not substantial or practical. In order to work for God, we must substantially and practically present our bodies to Him for His use. This is the way to be a consecrated person living to God.

2. "Present...your members as weapons of righteousness to God" (Rom. 6:13, see also v. 19).

It is not enough to present our bodies a living sacrifice in a general way. We must specifically present our members to God as weapons of righteousness. Each of our members should be presented to God for His use through our consecration. They should not be used as weapons of sin or the world. For example, if we use one of our members to sin, such as wearing an improper article of clothing, we allow our members to be weapons of sin or the world. Through consecration we must bring all our members back from sin and the world and give them to God for His use to do righteous acts and to serve Him. In this way, we glorify God in our members, which is to glorify God in our bodies.

Everything

1. "The firstborn" (Exo. 13:2).

The firstborn speaks of God's redemption (v. 15). God has the right to gain what He has redeemed. Therefore, we should present the firstborn to God. Furthermore, the firstborn represents what is strong. We should present what is strong to God.

2. "Your only son, whom you love" (Gen. 22:2).

The only begotten is the unique one; the beloved is the most dear. We should consecrate these things to God. If our consecration does not touch what is most precious to our hearts, it is too superficial. We should present our unique and most beloved thing.

3. "The first of the fruit" (Deut. 26:10).

We should consecrate the first of the fruit, that is, the things that are first. We should not present the things that are last to the Lord.

4. "The best" (Num. 18:12).

We should present the best to the Lord. The Lord always touches our best things. He always contends with us over the things we consider best and important. There was once a mother who had three sons. The eldest was very bright, so she told him to study medicine. The second son also was bright, so she told him to study business. However, the third son was very stupid, so she told him to enter a seminary and become a preacher. It should not be this way. The best should be offered to God. Mr. George Müller once stayed in a brother's home, and he noticed that this brother rose up very early every morning to touch the Lord. He asked him why he needed to get up so early. The brother said that in the Old Testament God required people to offer the fat of the offering, not the dung. (The fat was the best part of the offering, and the dung was the worst.) We must give our best time to the Lord. Indeed, we should consecrate the best to the Lord.

5. "Your substance" (Prov. 3:9).

Since our person is consecrated to the Lord, our substance, our money, should also be offered up. If we do not present our money, there is a problem with our consecration.

6. "All" (Luke 21:4).

We should offer up our all. Throughout the ages, the Lord has used those who offered up their all. They spent their money and strength for the Lord and the gospel. If a person truly loves the Lord, he must love Him to such an extent that he puts forth everything for the Lord. If we love the Lord, we will not hold anything back. When the Lord comes, all things must go.

HOW TO CONSECRATE

Voluntarily

1. "Of their own accord" (2 Cor. 8:3).

The Lord is precious. He is worthy of our consecration. Therefore, our consecration must be voluntary. We devalue the Lord with an involuntary consecration.

2. "As a blessing and not as a matter of covetousness...Each one as he has purposed in his heart, not out of sorrow or out of necessity, for God loves a cheerful giver" (2 Cor. 9:5, 7).

God never forces people to consecrate; it is a matter of our free will. God loves a cheerful giver.

In Secret

1. "Do not sound a trumpet before you...Do not let your left hand know...Be in secret" (Matt. 6:2-4).

Our consecration should be in secret. We should not advertise it before man, that is, to "sound a trumpet." We should not let people know, lest we receive praise and glory from man but lose the reward from God. For the glory of God and the benefit of others, our consecration should be hidden, not revealed.

THE GOAL OF CONSECRATION

To Live to the Lord

1. "No longer live to themselves but to Him who died for them and has been raised" (2 Cor. 5:15).

The goal of consecration is to live to the Lord. This does not necessarily mean that we must become missionaries. It means that, according to the Lord's purpose and arrangement, we testify of the Lord and glorify Him in all that we do. Our whole living should be according to the Lord's will and pleasing to the Lord. The choice of our clothing and food, the spending of our money, the use of our time, the visiting of our friends, and everything in our living must be according to the Lord's heart's desire and to the Lord, not according to our own will and to ourselves. Such a person, even if he is not a missionary, will be living to the Lord. Although he may not be able to give a message, he will be able to live the Lord so that others can see the Lord in him and sense His presence.

To Be a Living Sacrifice

1. "Present your bodies a living sacrifice, holy, well pleasing to God" (Rom. 12:1).

A sacrifice is pleasing to God and satisfies Him. When we

present our bodies, we are a sacrifice to God. In the Old Testament people offered sacrifices that were dead. Today, however, we present our bodies to God as living sacrifices so that they may be used by God and work for God. This does not refer to "dedicating ourselves to be a missionary." It refers to presenting our bodies to be used by God according to His will to serve Him. Our body moves according to the leading of the Holy Spirit within us. In this way our body is a living sacrifice for God's use. Although God has no intention that all His children would be missionaries, He wants each of us to present our bodies as a living sacrifice to serve Him.

Once a sacrifice is offered to God, its activity and destiny are determined by God, not by itself. Once we present ourselves to God as a living sacrifice, we should act according to God rather than our own ideas. We must be limited by God and follow His will.

To Serve God

1. "Present your bodies...which is your reasonable service" (Rom. 12:1).

We present our bodies to God as a living sacrifice for serving Him. According to the context of Romans 12:1, this refers to our coordination in the service of the Body of Christ, the church. This should be the goal of our consecration.

To Follow the Will of God

1. "Present your bodies...that you may prove what the will of God is, that which is good and well pleasing and perfect" (Rom. 12:1-2).

Our real and proper service toward God must be in accordance with God's will. Therefore, since our consecration is to serve God, the goal of consecration must also be to follow His will.

To Let God Work

1. "We are His masterpiece, created in Christ Jesus for good works, which God prepared beforehand in order that we would walk in them" (Eph. 2:10).

Our consecration to God is not only for the purpose of

working for God but even more to allow God to work. We are not only God's workers but also His workmanship. As God's workers, we should work for God. As God's workmanship, we should let God work. We must let God work before we can work for God. God wants to work Himself and all that He has into us, so He has much work to do in us. This requires our cooperation. If God wanted to work on wood or stone, He would not need their cooperation, because they are not living. But when God wants to work on us, He needs our cooperation, because we have a mind, emotion, and will. Without our cooperation, He cannot do anything. Our cooperation is our consecration. When we consecrate ourselves to God, we express our willingness to let God work in us. From the time we were saved, He has been waiting for our consecration, waiting for us to hand ourselves over into His hand to let Him work in us. If we do not have this kind of consecration, God has no way to do the work that He wants to do in us. Therefore, we must give ourselves completely to God to allow Him to work in us as He pleases. The amount of work that we can do for God depends upon the amount of work that we allow Him to do in us. If we let Him work in us, He will work His riches into us by the Holy Spirit, and we will be able to work His riches into others by the Holy Spirit. Will we let Him work? The answer depends upon our consecration.

To Glorify God

1. "For you have been bought with a price. So then glorify God in your body" (1 Cor. 6:20).

The final goal of our consecration is to glorify God. To glorify God is to express God, to live Him out. The light shining out from a light bulb is its glory. We consecrate in order to put everything of ourselves aside and to let God become our everything so that He has the complete position within us to express Himself through us and to be glorified.

THE RESULTS OF CONSECRATION

Understanding the Will of God

1. "Present your bodies...prove what the will of God is" (Rom. 12:1-2).

The first result of consecration is that we can understand the will of God. Only those who are consecrated to God to live to Him can understand the will of God.

Being Able to Be Enlightened by the Lord

1. "Whenever their heart turns to the Lord, the veil is taken away" (2 Cor. 3:16).

The Lord is light. When our heart is turned from the Lord to something else, a veil covers us from His enlightenment. If our heart turns to the Lord, we can be enlightened in the light of His face. Turning to the Lord is our giving of ourselves to Him. It is a true consecration. Therefore, consecration can cause us to see the Lord's light. If we consecrate ourselves to the Lord from our heart, if we are turned toward the Lord, we will obtain His enlightening. Some brothers and sisters have no light because their heart has not been fully consecrated to the Lord. It is still attracted to things other than the Lord. Miss M. E. Barber said that a small leaf can cover the stars in the night. If we want light, we must have a complete consecration to take away every covering.

Being Able to Have Faith

1. "Commit your way to Jehovah, / And trust in Him" (Psa. 37:5).

We must commit our way to God in order to trust in Him. To commit is to consecrate. To trust is to believe. Therefore, only a consecrated person has faith. If we do not let go of ourselves and our matters and place them in the Lord's hands, we cannot believe that the Lord will be responsible for us.

Being Able to Have Spiritual Experiences

1. "Do not let sin therefore reign...Present yourselves to God...Sin will not lord it over you" (Rom. 6:12-14).

If we want to experience freedom from sin, we must consecrate ourselves to God.

2. "Present your members as slaves to righteousness unto sanctification" (Rom. 6:19).

We must present our members in order to experience

sanctification. This verse and the preceding verses prove that consecration enables us to have spiritual experiences. Prayer, faith, joy, peace, overcoming, sanctification, and being filled with the Holy Spirit for power are all experiences that come out of consecration. This is confirmed by the experiences and writings of many saints who have gone before us. In order to have any spiritual experience, we must be consecrated. Consecration is a crucial gate. To enter into the reality of any spiritual experience, we must pass through this gate. We cannot expect any kind of spiritual experience without consecration.

Enjoying All the Riches of the Lord's Glory

1. **"An acceptable sacrifice, well pleasing to God... God will fill your every need according to His riches, in glory, in Christ Jesus"** (Phil. 4:18-19; see also the verses related to the points above, "Enjoying What the Lord Has Prepared" and "Gaining the Lord's Blessing and Supply").

We enjoy all the riches of the Lord's glory through consecration. If we offer what is well pleasing to God, He will cause us to enjoy the riches of His glory.

Chapter Twenty-Four

DEALING WITH SIN

I. The meaning of dealing with sin:
   A. Producing fruits of repentance.
   B. Purging leaven.
II. Confessing sin:
   A. Confessing sin to God.
   B. Confessing sin to man.
III. Being reconciled to others.
IV. Making restoration to others.
V. Clearing up evil things.

THE MEANING OF DEALING WITH SIN

Producing Fruits of Repentance

1. "Produce then fruit worthy of your repentance" (Matt. 3:8; see also Acts 26:20).

As soon as we repent and believe in the Lord, we should produce fruits of repentance. There are both positive and negative aspects to this matter. In regard to the positive aspect, all our actions and behavior should be according to God's desire. In regard to the negative aspect, we should deal completely with the sins and wrongdoings that we committed in the past, and we should no longer participate in them. For example, before a brother repents and believes in the Lord, he may argue and even fight with his wife. After repenting, he should go to his wife and confess his wrongdoing in arguing and his sin of fighting with her. He should beg her forgiveness. In this way he can clear up any negative impression that his wife has toward him. Thus, he will produce fruits of repentance by dealing with the wrongdoings and sins that he committed in the past.

Purging Leaven

1. "Unleavened bread shall be eaten...and nothing leavened shall be seen with you, nor shall any leaven be seen with you in all your territory"; "Let us keep the feast, not with old leaven, neither with the leaven of malice and evil, but with the unleavened bread of sincerity and truth" (Exo. 13:7; 1 Cor. 5:8).

Dealing with sin is related to purging out leaven, which makes dough rise. In the Bible leaven does not refer to positive things. Instead, leaven refers to heresy (Matt. 16:12) and sins, both of which are negative things. The evil and uncleanness of leaven corrupt us. Therefore, we should completely purge it out.

In the Old Testament, God told the children of Israel to eat unleavened bread immediately following the Passover and to completely purge out the leaven from their surroundings. This type indicates that we must purge out any evil and unclean things from us and our surroundings once we are saved. Furthermore, we should no longer touch these things. The children of Israel kept the Feast of Unleavened Bread for seven days, which represents a complete period of time. This means that from the time that we are saved until we meet the Lord, we must purge out any leaven and live an unleavened life. We must purge out every evil action and deal with every unclean thing so that we may become and continue to be a new lump of dough. We should deal with sin as soon as we are saved and continue to deal with it until we meet the Lord.

CONFESSING SIN

Confessing Sin to God

1. "When I kept silent, my bones wasted away / Through my groaning all day long... / I acknowledged my sin to You, / And I did not cover my iniquity. / I said, I will confess my transgressions to Jehovah. / Then You forgave the iniquity of my sin. / ...You surround me with the ringing shouts of deliverance" (Psa. 32:3, 5, 7).

Dealing with sin includes several things. First, we should confess our sins both to God and to man. To confess our sins to God is to come before Him and to confess everything that we have done that offends Him. Every sin that we commit offends God, whether the sin is against God or against man. We may think that David sinned only against man and offended man when he usurped the wife of Uriah and had him killed, but David acknowledged that he had sinned against God and man (51:1-17). Therefore, David confessed his sin to God. Before he confessed his sin to God, he suffered, but when he did not hide his evil and confessed it to God, he was forgiven by God and surrounded with the ringing shouts of deliverance. This caused him to be full of joy. Thus, if we want the joy of salvation, we must confess our sins before God.

Many have repented and were saved but have never thoroughly confessed their sins before God. Therefore, they do not have much joy of salvation or spiritual hunger, thirst, pursuit, or growth. If we want to richly taste the Lord's joy of salvation, we must come before the Lord and thoroughly confess our sins. If we also want to have spiritual hunger, thirst, pursuit, and growth, we must come before God and confess our sins one by one. When we confess our sins to God in this way, we cannot be general; we cannot confess, in principle only, that we have sinned greatly. We must be specific and confess our sins one by one. We cannot bring a bag of sins to God, throw it down before Him, and forget about it. We must open the bag of sins before God and mention each sin; we must open the bag and thoroughly confess each sin one by one. It is not sufficient to say to God, "I have committed many sins. I am full of sin. Please forgive me," and think that everything is all right. We must ask God to search us, enlighten us, and expose all our sins so that we might see them and confess them to Him one by one. Only this is sufficient. When we pray to God in this way, He will enlighten us through the Holy Spirit and expose our previous sins one by one. He wants us to realize how we have offended our parents, brothers, and sisters; how we have wronged our wife or husband and children; and how we owe our teachers, fellow students, friends, relatives, and neighbors. He also wants us to realize how we cheated and stole from people, sought personal gain in public positions, profited at the expense of others, were falsely benevolent and falsely righteous, were evil in thoughts and devious in actions, and committed other sins and transgressions. If we let Him enlighten us, He will uncover all our sins and enlighten us. When we become aware of a sin, we should confess it to Him. We should confess our sins one by one until we feel that we do not need to confess anything more. If we practice this, we will be able to thoroughly confess our sins to God. This is not related to our salvation; it is related to our living after salvation. It is not a requirement for salvation but a condition for spiritual growth. Receiving of the Lord's salvation is not based on this kind of confession; however, those who have received the Lord's salvation should confess their sins in this way.

2. "If we confess our sins, He is faithful and righteous to forgive us our sins and cleanse us" (1 John 1:9).

Every saved one should confess his sins to God. If we sin

after we are saved, we should confess our sin to God to receive His forgiveness and cleansing. We should not have any unconfessed sins or transgressions before God. If many unconfessed transgressions pile upon us, our spirit will not be able to be released or bright. We should always confess our sins to God. We should completely deal with our sins before God at all times so that we do not lose our fellowship with Him but live in the light of His face. We should clear away the barriers between God and ourselves through the confession of our sins to recover and maintain our fellowship with Him.

3. "He who covers his transgressions will not prosper, / But whoever confesses and forsakes them will obtain mercy" (Prov. 28:13).

According to the ordinances of God, if we cover our sins, we will not prosper. If we confess and forsake our sins, however, we will receive God's mercy. If we want to receive God's mercy, we must confess our sins. Confessing our sins to God is a prerequisite for receiving mercy. If we do not completely confess our sins before God, we will lose His mercy and will not prosper.

If we want to experience the joy of our salvation, to remove the barriers between God and us in order to restore and maintain our fellowship with God, or to receive God's mercy and blessing, we must confess our sins to God. God hates sin. Sin prevents us from receiving His blessing and kills the spiritual things in us. We must completely deal with sin before God so that it will not touch us. We should practice this earnestly. The more thoroughly we deal with sin, the better.

Confessing Sin to Man

1. "Whoever confesses and forsakes them will obtain mercy" (Prov. 28:13).

Most of our sins offend others, so we should not only confess our sins to God but also to man. We confess our sins to God because every sin that we commit offends Him. However, the sins that we commit not only offend God but also man. If we offend God, He immediately forgives us when we confess our sins. But God's forgiveness cannot take care of the people whom we have offended. Therefore, we still must confess our sins to man. If we sin against and offend our neighbor, we need not only the forgiveness of God but also that of our neighbor. We need to confess to our neighbor and beg for forgiveness. Otherwise, even with God's forgiveness, we will still be condemned before our neighbor and our heart will be bound. If we want to be released and forgiven by our neighbor so that we can act freely before him, we must confess our sin to him. Proverbs 28 surely refers to confessing our sins to man.

2. "Confess your sins to one another" (James 5:16).

God wants us to confess our sins to one another. When we confess our sins to one another, we confess our sins to men. As we deal with each other as brothers and sisters, there are always matters in which others offend us or we offend others, so we must confess our sins to each other. If we commit a sin or make a mistake that offends a brother or sister, we should not only confess that sin to God but also to the brother or sister whom we offended. This will cause us to receive forgiveness from God and from the brother or sister.

3. "They shall confess their sin which they have committed" (Num. 5:7).

According to the context of this verse, confessing sin refers to confessing to God and to the offended person. When we are negligent in our obligations to man and offend God, we must confess our sins to God and to the affected person so that the matter can be cleared up. God does not want us to be sinful and unrighteous before Him nor to be sinful and unrighteous before men. Therefore, He wants us to confess our sins to Him, and He also wants us to confess our sins to man.

As children of God, we should completely confess our sins before God and completely deal with our sins before man. Although this is not related to our salvation, it is very much related to our spiritual growth. No Christian can have spiritual growth without confessing sins and dealing with them before man in this way. There once was a revival meeting in England. A believer came and asked the leader of the meeting, "How can Christians grow?" The leader of the meeting asked, "How long has it been since you confessed your sins to others?" When the believer first heard this word, he was surprised. He wondered how confessing sins to others could help a Christian grow in life. Later he realized that confessing sins to others not only enables a Christian to grow but is also a basic requirement for Christian growth.

Oh, brothers and sisters, a Christian who has never confessed sins to others is almost certainly a Christian who has never grown in life! If we want to know whether or not we have grown, we need only to look at whether or not we have confessed our sins to others. The amount that we grow is determined by the amount that we confess our sins. Confession of sins to others and growth are in direct proportion to one another. They have a mutual cause-and-effect relationship. Confessing sins to others not only causes us to grow, but our growth requires and causes us to confess our sins to others. If we are continuously growing, we certainly are continuously confessing our sins to others.

Confessing our sins to others also causes our spirit to be released, revived, strengthened, and enlivened. The spirits of many brothers and sisters are not released and are in a dry, weak, and deadened condition because they have offended others and are unwilling to confess their sins to those whom they have offended. Sin deadens our spirit. This is especially true of the sins that offend others. Such sins cause the witness of our conscience in our spirit to be one of offense before man. Such sins hinder our spirit from rising up before others and keep it deadened and low. If we want our spirit to be released and strong before others, we must confess our sins to man to remove the offense in our conscience.

When we confess our sins to others, we should not be afraid to be conscientious and thorough. The more conscientious we are and the more thorough we are, the more benefit we will gain. Furthermore, we should not hesitate or wait. We should take advantage of the first opportunity and do our best to confess things quickly. In 1933, when I was thoroughly enlightened and cleansed by God, I sent forty letters in one day to confess my sins to people, apologize, and beg their forgiveness. Looking back, I realize that that day had a great impact on the amount of grace that I have since received in the Lord's way. Praise the Lord that He gave me the grace to conscientiously deal with the matters in which I had offended people.

In confessing our sins to others, we must pay attention to the extent of our confession. In principle, the extent to which we have offended others should be the extent of our confession to others. It should not be greater or less. We should confess our sin to whomever we have offended. We should confess our sins to as many people as we have offended. We should not confess to more people or confess to fewer people. If we confess to fewer people, we still owe some an apology. If we confess to more people than necessary, it creates a problem. We should not confess an offense to someone whom we have not offended, because it makes them aware of our sin unnecessarily. The purpose of confessing our sins is to erase the impression of our sin among those whom we have offended. If our confessing instead causes someone with no knowledge of our sin to gain an impression of it, such a confession is improper.

Our confession of sins not only gives us blessings but also glorifies God and benefits others. If our confession of sin to others does not glorify God or benefit others, even if it may cause us to receive blessing, we should not do it. Thus, we should have wisdom in the matter of confessing sins to men. We should do it in a way that glorifies God and benefits others. We must not shame God's name or cause others to suffer loss because of our confession of sins.

BEING RECONCILED TO OTHERS

1. "Therefore if you are offering your gift...and there you remember that your brother has something against you...first go and be reconciled to your brother... Be well disposed quickly with your opponent at law, while you are with him on the way" (Matt. 5:23-25).

Second, dealing with sin involves being reconciled to others. Confessing sins to others involves begging others' forgiveness for offending them. Being reconciled to others involves going and seeking peace with those who have animosity toward us. These two aspects are connected because those whom we have offended often hold a grudge against us.

Therefore, we need to beg for forgiveness and seek peace with them. Sometimes, however, we are blamed for something by others, even when we have not offended them. In such a situation, we do not need to beg for forgiveness, but we should seek peace. We should do this so that no problem exists between ourselves and others or between others and ourselves. This enables us to be bold, and it eliminates all barriers when we come close to God and have fellowship with Him. (The offering of our gift in Matthew 5 refers to fellowship with God.)

2. **"When you stand praying, forgive, if you have anything against anyone"** (Mark 11:25).

If we have offended anyone, we should confess our sins to him and beg for forgiveness. This verse, however, says that we should forgive anyone who has offended us. If we want to live before God, we must do more than beg forgiveness from those we have offended; we must also forgive those who have offended us. Regardless of whether we have offended others or others have offended us, we must clear up any offense so that there is no separation between them and us before God. Then there will be no barriers to our prayer or barriers to the answers to our prayer. Any separation between others and us blocks our prayer and becomes a barrier to receiving an answer to prayer. Therefore, we must deal with these things completely so that we would not be separated from God.

Forgiving others is often harder than begging for forgiveness. Perhaps this is the reason that the Bible constantly teaches us to forgive others. The Lord often connected forgiving others with prayer because if we do not forgive others, God will not forgive us, and there will be a separation between God and us. This will break our fellowship with God, and we will be unable to pray to God in an unhindered way. Moreover, we will be unable to receive God's answer. We may not have offended others or created problems with them, and we may not need to beg forgiveness of others or clear up matters, but whenever someone offends us, if we do not forgive him from the heart, we will have a problem with him, and this matter will block our fellowship with God. Since it will interrupt our prayer to God, we must deal with it by forgiving others.

MAKING RESTORATION TO OTHERS

1. "If anyone sins and acts unfaithfully against Jehovah and deceives his associate in regard to a deposit or a security, or by robbery, or has extorted from his associate, or has found a lost item and lied about it, if he has sworn falsely in any one of all these things a man may do and sins thereby...he shall even restore it in full, and shall add to it a fifth part of it. He shall give it to the one to whom it belongs, on the day he is found guilty" (Lev. 6:2-3, 5).

Third, we should deal with sin by restoring money to those whom we have cheated. If we have cheated others in money matters, we should repay the principal with an additional fifth part as soon as we realize our transgression. Although this is an ordinance of the Old Testament law, the principle still applies in the New Testament. In the New Testament the work of grace on a person has a higher requirement than that of the Old Testament. When the tax collector Zaccheus was saved, he said, "If I have taken anything from anyone by false accusation, I restore four times as much" (Luke 19:8). This was the work of the Lord's grace on him. Although we need not regard Zaccheus as a standard, we must at least comply with the requirement of the law, which is to return the amount in question with an additional fifth part.

Brothers and sisters, whether we owe something to the government or to individual persons, we should restore it all. If we do not, we will have unrighteous things in our hands or in our home. We cannot merely confess our sin of cheating people to God and then forget about it. We must completely restore what we cheated from others. When we confess our sin of cheating people to God, He will forgive us, but we still need to resolve the matter involved in our cheating of others. If something we obtained unrighteously is still in our hands, it will give us a feeling of unrighteousness and will interrupt our progress in spiritual matters. Can we read the Bible on a table that was bought with money obtained unrighteously? Can we kneel in prayer before a bed that we gained improperly? Can we give a message wearing a suit that was acquired unrighteously? God forgives all our sins when we believe in the Lord and when we confess them, but there is still a need to make restoration and completely deal with any unrighteous thing that is still in our hands. Although this has no relationship to our salvation, it is very much related to our spiritual life following our salvation. This would be like living with the corpse of a person of whose murder you have been absolved. Even if you have been absolved of his murder, you would have a difficult time living a comfortable life if the corpse was not removed from your house. Everything gained by unrighteous, improper means is like an unremoved corpse; it hinders us from living a comfortable spiritual life. Therefore, we must completely clear away everything of unrighteous gain and return it in a proper way.

This kind of restoration pleases God and is a result of the special work of the Holy Spirit. In England many years ago F. B. Meyer was preaching. Without warning, he pointed to the audience and said, "Look, here is a young man who stole three pounds eighteen shillings from his master. If he does not return it, he will never have peace." The next day a young man came to see Meyer and said, "I am the person you talked about yesterday. I really did steal three pounds eighteen shillings from my master, and since then I have not had peace in my heart. With this check I will return the entire amount." This shows that the Holy Spirit does a special work to cause people to deal with matters in which they cheated others.

When God leads us to deal with these kinds of things, He also gives us some special experiences. Before I believed in the Lord, there was a fire where I worked. While everybody was moving things out of the building, I saw a small Chinese ink bottle and a brush. I liked both of them and stole them. After being saved, the Holy Spirit told me to deal with this unrighteous matter. At that time I still had the ink bottle, but I no longer had the small brush, so I could only use money to replace it. I took the small ink bottle and a dollar and went to my old boss. I shamefacedly confessed that I had stolen two things and said that I had come to make restoration. My boss listened but refused to take them. After I continued to beg him, he said, "I will take the ink bottle, but I will not take the money." Then he saw that I was carrying a small combined solar-lunar calendar card. At that time, everybody liked this kind of calendar card, but they were not easy to obtain. Then he said, "You can give me the calendar card as a substitute for the little brush." Although I did not want to give up my calendar card, I owed him, and so I had to agree. After I left his office, I felt sad about losing the calendar card, and I did not know what to do with the dollar. Inwardly I said, "The best thing would be for the Lord to show me a needy beggar so that I can give this dollar to him." When I arrived home, it was already dark, and I closed the door very securely because it was wartime. Not long afterward, there was a knock on the door. I opened the door to see who it was. It was a beggar who could not find anything to eat. He came to ask for help. I felt that God answered my request, so I brought him in, fed him, and gave him a few steamed rolls. He did not know where to look for lodging, so I agreed to take him to a place. On the way, I gave him the dollar and told him that it was from the Lord Jesus. At a crossroads I pointed to a place where he could stay. He thanked me and left. At that moment Brother Chao Ching Hwai called to me from across the street, "Brother Lee, where are you going?" He came across the street, and I told him what had happened. He took an envelope and handed it to me, saying, "This is a gift for you." When I arrived home and opened the envelope, I saw that it was a solar-lunar combined calendar card! By this time, I clearly understood God's leading. God gave me a special beggar so that I could deal with that dollar. Then He caused me to meet that brother so that He could restore the calendar card. Although these were small matters, God's arrangement and leading was truly marvelous! This proves that repaying our debts and dealing with unrighteous things pleases God.

2. "But if the man has no kinsman to whom restitution may be made for the wrong, the restitution which is made for the wrong goes to Jehovah for the priest" (Num. 5:8).

If we owe restitution for unrighteous things to a person who has died, we must make restitution to the relatives. If he has no kinsmen to receive our restitution, it should go to Jehovah for the priest. Today this means that it should go to the church.

We should make restitution in monetary matters within the limitations of our ability and circumstances. If we do not have the ability, or if our situation does not permit, it will be all right if we cannot do it. If we have the ability and the situation permits, we should be diligent in clearing up the matter. We should always clear up things to the best of our ability and to the extent that our circumstances permit so that our conscience will release us. We should do as much as we are able and as much as our circumstances permit us to do. If we truly are unable to repay the person whom we owe, we should still confess to him, beg his forgiveness, and promise to repay as soon as possible.

CLEARING UP EVIL THINGS

1. "He removed the foreign altars and the high places and smashed the pillars and hewed down the Asherahs"; "Purge...the Asherahs and the idols and the molten images" (2 Chron. 14:3; 34:3).

Fourth, in dealing with sin, we need to clear up evil things. We should remove every idol and everything used in the worship of idols. Many of us previously worshipped idols. After being saved, we should remove everything associated with their worship from our hands and our homes. If we hold on to these things, the devil has the ground to harass, attack, and disturb us. Therefore, we must clear up these things. We must completely stand on God's side, not leaving any little thing of the devil.

2. "A considerable number of those who practiced magic brought their books together and burned them before all; and they counted up the price of them and found it to be fifty thousand pieces of silver" (Acts 19:19).

We should also clean out devilish and immoral things. The believers in Ephesus burned many evil books. A few years ago I went to Wei Hai to preach the gospel. Those who were saved brought many demonic and filthy things to the meeting place and burned them in front of everyone. They made a good testimony and gained the joy of being freed from sin. Demonic books, obscene books, pornographic pictures, gambling apparatus, things related to smoking and drinking, and things related to other kinds of sin should be completely removed from our homes and possessions after we are saved. Regrettably, many brothers and sisters still have evil things and keep evil things on their person and in their homes. According to the Bible, for example, the dragon is a symbol of Satan (Rev. 20:2), but even now some brothers and sisters wear clothing, shoes, and jewelry with dragons on them, have dragon furniture, or use utensils with dragons on them. Even now some brothers and sisters have pornographic books on their bookshelves and hang superstitious writings or indecent pictures in their homes. These should be eliminated to testify that we are children of God. When we preached the gospel in 1938 in Beijing, an elderly sister asked me if it was all right for her to have a lampshade with a dragon on it. I asked her, "How do you feel inwardly?" She said, "I think there is a problem." I said, "Since you feel that there is a problem, why do you not take care of it?" So she got rid of the lampshade. If we truly want the Lord, the Holy Spirit will cause us to feel that certain things are wrong. We should not have any symbol of Satan on our person, in our homes, or on anything we own.

3. "If you return to the Almighty, you will be built up. / If you put injustice far away from your tents" (Job 22:23).

If we truly turn to God and desire to please Him, we must eliminate every evil and unrighteous thing from our person and homes. By doing this we can be built up before God.

If we practice what we have seen item by item and completely deal with every unrighteous and unclean thing and if we clear up everything until we are clean, we will have a strong testimony and walk in the straight way. God will bless us.

CHAPTER TWENTY-FIVE

BEING LED BY THE LORD

I. The kinds of leading:
  A. The teaching of the anointing.
  B. The leading of the Holy Spirit.
  C. The forbidding of the Holy Spirit.
  D. A gentle, quiet voice.
  E. The leading of the Lord's eye.
  F. The enlightenment of the Holy Spirit.
  G. Dreams and visions.
  H. The direction of our situation.
  I. The restraining of bit and bridle.
II. How to be led:
  A. Turning our hearts to the Lord.
  B. Opening to the Lord.
  C. Wanting the Lord with a pure heart.
  D. Fearing God.
  E. Trusting in God.
  F. Abiding in the Lord.
  G. Being close to the Lord and open to Him.
  H. Hearing the Lord's voice.
  I. Hearing the Lord's word.
  J. Comparing the revelation that we obtain with the Lord's word.
  K. Taking the Lord's word as our standard.
  L. Enduring sufferings.
  M. Obeying the Lord's leading concerning the first step.
III. The results of being led:
  A. Being filled and resting.
  B. Walking in the paths of righteousness.

Being led is a necessary part of the Christian life and service before God. Thus, we need to consider this topic carefully.

THE KINDS OF LEADING

The Bible shows that the Lord uses many marvelous ways to lead us. There are at least nine kinds of leading in the Bible.

The Teaching of the Anointing

1. "The anointing which you have received from Him abides in you, and you have no need that anyone teach you; but as His anointing teaches you concerning all things" (1 John 2:27).

The Lord leads us in a subjective way: He lives in us and leads us. The Lord's anointing lives in us and teaches us concerning all things. This is His leading. In chapter 21 we saw that the anointing spoken of in 1 John 2:27 refers to the moving of the Holy Spirit within us. The Holy Spirit moves within us like an ointment. He anoints us with the Lord's intention and causes us to know the things of God. Thus, the anointing within us, which is the moving of the Holy Spirit, teaches us concerning all things so that we may know the Lord's desire and be led by Him.

The anointing does not teach us only occasionally. It abides in us and teaches us constantly. It does not come into us for a moment and then leave. It abides in us forever; therefore, it teaches us constantly. It does not teach us about only a few things; it teaches us concerning all things. Since the Lord's anointing continuously teaches concerning all things, we do not need anyone to teach us. If we would accept the teaching of the anointing at every time, in every place, and concerning all things, we truly would have no need for anyone to teach us. Regardless of whether the teaching of the anointing concerns God, man, mundane affairs, important events, material things, or spiritual matters, as long as we are willing to receive its teaching, it will teach us inwardly.

The most precious thing about being a Christian is to receive the teaching of the anointing within us and to walk according to this inner anointing. When brothers and sisters have a problem, they often ask others for advice in order to be taught by them. This shows that they are outward Christians. But the Lord wants us to abide in Him, to fellowship with Him, and to receive the teaching of His anointing concerning all things and thus be inward Christians. Merely consulting others and being taught by them does not have much spiritual value. We must contact the Lord inwardly and receive the teaching of the anointing directly. This is precious. If we live this way, we can truly experience the reality of not needing anyone to teach us. The Lord's anointing will teach us in everything. Then we can fellowship with the Lord at any time and in any place, and no matter what we are doing, we will sense the teaching of the anointing.

The Leading of the Holy Spirit

1. "Led by the Spirit of God" (Rom. 8:14).

One of the most powerful ways in which the Lord leads us is by the leading of the Holy Spirit. We should focus more on the Holy Spirit than on natural or supernatural things. The Lord always leads us through the Holy Spirit. Although His leading seems to occur in conjunction with natural things, the leading of the Lord through the Holy Spirit often is unrelated to natural things; it is something spiritual, which we feel directly in our spirit.

The Forbidding of the Holy Spirit

1. "Having been forbidden by the Holy Spirit...the Spirit of Jesus did not allow them" (Acts 16:6-7).

The phrases *forbidden by the Holy Spirit* and *the Spirit of Jesus did not allow them* are like the two rails of a railroad track. When a train stays on its track, everything is normal. When we follow the two rails of the forbidding and restricting of the Holy Spirit within us, we feel very normal. Whenever we leave the railroad track of the Holy Spirit's leading, however, we no longer feel normal. Instead, we feel an inward forbidding and restricting. Brothers and sisters, whenever we feel that something is wrong, we need to be sensitive to the Holy Spirit's forbidding and restricting. For example, we may want to go to the house of a brother or sister, but when we arrive at the door and are about to ring the bell, we may inwardly sense that something is wrong. We should obey this feeling, refrain from ringing the door bell, and go home.

There was once a man in England who was much used by the Lord. On one occasion some people planned to trap him. They wrote a false letter and asked him to come to their house to help solve a spiritual problem. He went to the address in the letter, but as he was standing at the door, he felt a strong inward forbidding. Rather than ringing the bell, he turned around and went home. Later he learned about the trap that had been prepared for him. The Lord's inward forbidding stopped him and saved him. Oh, how precious is this forbidding! If we live in the Lord and follow Him, the Holy Spirit will often use this kind of forbidding and restricting to preserve us on God's track so that we can act according to God's will. If we are about to go against God's will, the Holy Spirit within us will not allow us. His forbidding and restricting are one way of the Lord's leading.

A Gentle, Quiet Voice

1. "My sheep hear My voice...and they follow Me" (John 10:27, see also v. 16).

The Lord Jesus' sheep hear His voice and follow Him. Therefore, the Lord's voice also leads us so that we may follow Him. We belong to the Lord, and we should pay attention to His voice and follow Him according to His voice.

2. "A great, strong wind...an earthquake...a fire... And after the fire, a gentle, quiet voice...came to him and said" (1 Kings 19:11-13).

Elijah's experience shows that the Lord speaks to His followers in a gentle, quiet voice. It is not a powerful voice like a great wind or an earthquake or a fire. The Lord was not in the great wind, the earthquake, or the fire. He was in the gentle, quiet voice that spoke to Elijah. Today the Lord often speaks to us and leads us with a gentle, quiet voice through the Holy Spirit within us. We should not look to the Lord to speak to us outwardly through miracles and great events. He directs us inwardly through a gentle, quiet voice.

The Leading of the Lord's Eye

1. "I will instruct you and teach you concerning the way you should go; / I will counsel you; my eye is upon you" (Psa. 32:8).

What is spoken of here is marvelous. The Lord instructs those who come near to Him and teaches them the way that they should go by guiding them with His eye. This kind of leading is very intimate. It is not expressed with words but with the expression of the eyes. For example, when we go to someone's home, the husband may simply look at his wife, who then knows that she should serve tea. This kind of communication is possible only between people who are close to one another.

The Enlightenment of the Holy Spirit

1. "Your word is a lamp to my feet / And a light to my path" (Psa. 119:105).

The Bible is the Lord's word to us. In principle it reveals the Lord's will to us in everything. Therefore, the Bible often enlightens us, lighting our steps in our way of following the Lord. This is another way that He leads us.

In ancient times when people went out at night on a dark road, they carried a torch to light their path. Wherever they walked, they had light. If they did not go to a certain place, the light did not go there either. Spiritually speaking, we are living in the night, and the Bible is like a torch—a lamp—that lights our way. The lamp is a light to our feet and to our path. It is for our walking, and it shines on our steps. If we do not walk in God's way, we will not be enlightened by the Bible. If we do not walk in God's way with our feet, and instead only use our mind to read God's Word, we will not gain light. God's Word shines forth light when our feet walk in God's way. Step by step, the Word is a lamp to our feet. Wherever we go, the Word of God enlightens us.

We must read the Bible carefully to discover its principles as the standard for our living and being. We must not use the Bible as if it were a fortune-telling book. Rather than reading the Bible consistently, some people open the Bible only when they have a problem. Then they pray a little and randomly point to a page. They regard whatever word that they point to as the Lord's direction and leading. This is superstitious and can sometimes be very dangerous. A person once opened the Bible and pointed to the words in Matthew 27:5 about Judas, which said, "He went away and hanged himself." It is easy to see how dangerous this method could be. Do you think that he should have hung himself? Sometimes this method can also produce very coincidental results. Once there was a brother in Fukien who did not know whether he should go to Southeast Asia to work for the Lord. He opened the Bible and pointed to the words in Acts 8:26 which said, "Go south." Despite the coincidence, do you think that this leading was reliable? The Bible should not be used this way. We should read its clear teachings and understand them, or we should learn its principles as our guide. Deuteronomy 22:10 says that an ox and a donkey should not be yoked together. In principle, this means that those who are clean should not be yoked with those who are unclean. By this we know that God does not permit those who have been cleansed by faith to cooperate with or to be yoked together with unclean unbelievers in anything, including marriage, business, or other matters. Therefore, in order to use the Bible as our guide in living, acting, or working before God, we must read the Bible carefully and then understand and apply it according to our proper understanding. This is the way of one who truly follows the Lord and is led by Him.

Dreams and Visions

1. "God speaks in one way, / Indeed in two ways, without any perceiving it— / In a dream, a night vision, / When deep sleep falls upon men... / Then He opens the ears of men / And seals up their instruction" (Job 33:14-16).

Sometimes the Lord leads us with dreams and visions. These verses indicate that God speaks in one way, indeed in two ways, without man perceiving it; consequently, God uses dreams and visions to open man's ears and to instruct him. Dreams and visions are not a primary means of His leading but a secondary one. In His leading, God primarily speaks to men. If men do not understand His word, He can use dreams and visions to direct them. If God speaks to men in one way, indeed in two ways, and they still do not perceive, God is forced to use dreams and visions to instruct them. Therefore, we should place more emphasis on God's word than on dreams and visions. Today there is a group of people who pays too much attention to dreams and visions. They neglect the Word of God and emphasize instead the seeking of dreams and visions. When they meet, one will say that he had a dream, and another will claim to have seen a vision. Dreams and visions easily attract people's attention. Curious people especially like these things. But a normal follower of the Lord always places the Lord's word first. Of course, we do acknowledge that the Lord does give dreams and visions to direct and lead us or to comfort and strengthen us when necessary. I have been graced by the Lord in this way and have had this kind of experience, but we should regard the Lord's word as the most important thing.

2. "Having been forbidden by the Holy Spirit...the Spirit of Jesus did not allow them...A vision appeared to Paul during the night...And when he had seen the vision...concluding that God had called us to announce the gospel to them" (Acts 16:6-7, 9-10).

These verses and the verses in Job 33 are very similar. When Paul went out to preach the gospel, he wanted to stay in Asia, but the Holy Spirit forbade him. He wanted to go to Bithynia, but the Spirit of Jesus did not allow him. By looking at a map, we can see that the Holy Spirit wanted him to cross the Aegean Sea and go to Macedonia on the opposite side. However, Paul did not understand this at the time. It was as if God was speaking to him one way, indeed in two ways, but he did not perceive it. This forced God to use a vision in the night to direct him, which also shows that this kind of leading is not primary but secondary. Paul's primary leading was the speaking or sense from God given to him by the Holy Spirit.

We should also pay attention to Paul's response to the vision. After Paul saw the vision, he concluded that God had called him to bring the good news to Macedonia. He did not believe it until he had carefully considered the vision. We should not believe dreams and visions lightly. If we have a dream or vision and believe it without any discernment or consideration, we can be easily cheated.

The Direction of Our Situation

1. "Jacob heard the words of Laban's sons...And Jacob saw Laban's countenance, and now it was not favorable toward him as previously. And Jehovah said to Jacob, Return to the land of your fathers" (Gen. 31:1-3).

A Christian must be able to understand the speaking that he receives from the Bible outwardly, the Holy Spirit inwardly, and the situation around him. Our situation often is a hint or proof of the Lord's leading. Jacob heard Laban's sons talking about him in the house. Then he saw that Laban's countenance was not favorable toward him. Spontaneously, he felt he should no longer stay in Laban's house. At this point, God spoke to him, saying, "Return to the land of your fathers." Thus, he was clear that he should leave. If we want to be led by the Lord, we must also understand our situation and pay attention to the meaning of its direction. The direction of our situation also serves as a leading from the Lord.

The Restraining of Bit and Bridle

1. "Do not be like a horse or like a mule, without understanding; / Whose trappings consist of bit and bridle to restrain them, / Else they do not come near you" (Psa. 32:9).

Horses and mules are without understanding. They often do not obey their handlers. Therefore, the handler uses a bit and bridle to restrain them and make them obey. Before the Lord we sometimes do not obey. This forces the Lord to use hard situations to deal with us and to lead us. These hard situations are the bit and bridle used by the Lord to restrain us and cause us to obey His leading. The restraining of horses and mules by bit and bridle causes obedience through pain. The hardships of the Lord's dealing produce similar pains to us. This kind of situational dealing, which restrains us through hardships, is a leading of the Lord to us.

HOW TO BE LED

It is useless to know about the Lord's leading but not know how to be led by the Lord. Therefore, we must not only know about the Lord's leading, but we must also know how to be led by the Lord. Knowing about the Lord's leading is objective; knowing how to be led by the Lord is subjective. We must consider how to be led by the Lord because it is more important than only knowing about the Lord's leading.

Turning Our Hearts to the Lord

1. "Whenever their heart turns to the Lord, the veil is taken away" (2 Cor. 3:16).

The Lord's leading cannot be separated from the Lord Himself. We can even say that the Lord Himself is His leading. A person whose heart is turned away from the Lord definitely cannot be led by the Lord. If we want to be led by the Lord, we must turn to the Lord. If we do not see the Lord's leading, it is because our heart is away from the Lord, and this becomes a veil covering our eyes. Whenever our heart turns to the Lord, this veil is taken away. When we are unveiled before the Lord, we can easily see the Lord's light and be led by the Lord.

Opening to the Lord

1. "We all with unveiled face, beholding...the glory of the Lord" (2 Cor. 3:18).

If we want to receive the Lord's leading, we must see the light of the Lord's face, and if we want to see the light of the Lord's face, we must open to the Lord. A person who is closed to the Lord cannot see the light of His face and receive His leading. We must open to the Lord from our innermost part without any hint of being closed. Then we can enter into the light of the Lord's face and see the direction of the Lord and receive His leading.

Wanting the Lord with a Pure Heart

1. "The pure in heart...shall see God" (Matt. 5:8).

God is light; therefore, those who see God are easily

enlightened and led. If we want to see God, we must be pure in heart. In the Bible being pure in heart means that we are single and simple toward God. We want God Himself and nothing other than God. If we want God and something other than God, loving both God and the world, our heart will not be single, simple, and pure toward Him. Once our heart is not pure or single toward God, our eyes will not be single either. They will be evil. The Lord said, "If therefore your eye is single, your whole body will be full of light; but if your eye is evil, your whole body will be dark" (6:22-23). If our heart is not pure toward God, our eye will be evil and our whole being will be dark. How can we be led by the Lord in such a condition? If we want to be led by the Lord, we must desire the Lord with a pure heart. Desiring the Lord with a pure heart is an important condition of being led by the Lord.

Fearing God

1. **"Who then is the man who fears Jehovah? / Him will He instruct concerning the way that he should choose"** (Psa. 25:12).

Fearing God is also a requirement of being led by the Lord. To fear God is to be afraid of offending God. It is not only to fear sin and worldliness but even more to fear ourselves. The real fear of God is to be afraid of ourselves. It is to be afraid of bringing anything of ourselves into the things of God—any element of ourselves, our likes, our opinions, and our choices. If we fear God in this way and reject ourselves, God will instruct us in the way that we should choose, and we will receive His leading.

2. **"The intimate counsel of Jehovah is to those who fear Him, / And His covenant will He make known to them"** (Psa. 25:14).

If we fear God, we will be afraid of offending Him, so we will reject ourselves and all that is offensive to God in everything that we do. Then we will receive more than God's ordinary leading; we will know the intimate counsel of God. The intimate counsel of God will be with us, and He will show us His covenant.

Trusting in God

1. "Trust in Jehovah with all your heart, / And do not rely on your own understanding; / In all your ways acknowledge Him, / And He will make your paths straight" (Prov. 3:5-6).

The Lord does not lead those who think that they are clever or who rely on their own cleverness. The Lord can only lead and direct the paths of those who reject their own cleverness and trust in the Lord with all their heart and who acknowledge Him in all their ways.

Abiding in the Lord

1. "His anointing teaches you concerning all things... and even as it has taught you, abide in Him" (1 John 2:27).

Abiding in the Lord and receiving the teaching of His anointing are absolutely related. On the one hand, we must obey the teaching of the anointing to abide in the Lord. On the other hand, we must abide in the Lord to receive the teaching of the anointing. To abide in the Lord is to fellowship with the Lord without any barriers. If a barrier between the Lord and us breaks our fellowship, how can we receive the teaching of the anointing? Those who receive the teaching of the anointing are those who abide in the Lord and fellowship with Him. If we want to be led by the Lord, we must deal with any barriers between the Lord and us in order to recover and maintain our fellowship with the Lord and to abide in Him.

If we want to abide in the Lord, receive the teaching of the anointing, and gain the Lord's leading, we must be quiet in our spirit. The Lord's anointing within us is the moving of the Holy Spirit. It is always gentle. If we are rough, hurried, or excited, it is not easy for us to feel the anointing. Inwardly, we must be steady, quiet, and gentle to feel the moving of the Holy Spirit, to receive the teaching of the anointing, and to be led by the Lord.

Being Close to the Lord and Open to Him

1. "I will counsel you; my eye is upon you" (Psa. 32:8).

God's intimate leading with His eye requires that we be close to and open to God. If we are far from Him, we will not see how He is leading us with His eye. We must be close to Him. However, being close is not enough; we must also be open to Him. If there is a barrier between Him and us, we cannot see what He is saying with His eye, no matter how close we are. Being close but not open means that we cannot see at all. I can be very close to you, but if there is a piece of paper between us, I cannot see your eyes. Therefore, we need to be close to and also open to the Lord. There should be no distance between us, and there should be no barriers. Only then will we be able to receive the intimate leading of His eye.

Hearing the Lord's Voice

1. "My sheep hear My voice...and they follow Me" (John 10:27).

To be led by the Lord, we must also be able to hear the Lord's voice. Because the Lord's voice is gentle and quiet, we need to be quiet in order to hear it. We must not only be quiet outwardly, but even more we must be quiet inwardly because the Lord's voice, which is gentle and quiet, is also within us. To hear the Lord's voice, we must not only be at peace, but even more we must be inwardly peaceful. We must learn to constantly return to our inner being and listen to the Lord's voice—His gentle, quiet voice—in a peaceful condition so that we can be led by Him. If we seek to hear the Lord's voice outwardly, we will be deceived by the falsehood of Satan's evil spirits. This kind of deceit actually occurred previously in Fukien.

Hearing the Lord's Word

1. "He awakens me morning by morning; / He awakens my ear / To hear as an instructed one" (Isa. 50:4).

Being able to hear the Lord's word is very much related to being led by the Lord. We should learn to come before the Lord every morning as an instructed one looking to Him to speak to us. We should ask the Lord to awaken our ears to hear His word. Although the Bible is the Lord's word, it is written in black and white letters. Prayer is needed in order to make it fresh and living so that He can give us His direction and leading each day.

Comparing the Revelation That We Obtain with the Lord's Word

1. "We saw His star at its rising...So it is written through the prophet" (Matt. 2:2, 5).

When the magi from the east first saw Christ's star, they obtained a revelation of His birth, but they did not know where Christ would be born. When they compared their revelation to the Old Testament, they knew He would be born in Bethlehem. We often have an inward sense from the Lord and even obtain a revelation from Him, but we must compare this revelation to the Scriptures to clearly understand the Lord's meaning. Therefore, we must be very familiar with the Bible so that we can compare it to our sense from Him in order to understand His revelations and be led by Him.

Taking the Lord's Word as Our Standard

1. "To the law and to the testimony! If they do not speak according to this word, it is because in them there is no dawn" (Isa. 8:20).

In being led by the Lord in various matters, we must absolutely take the Lord's Word—the Bible—as our standard. Even if a sense of leading comes from a feeling, a dream or vision, the direction of our situation, a teaching that we received from someone, or something that we read in a book, it still must be according to the Lord's Word in order for us to receive it and to understand His leading. If it is not according to the Bible, it will not be reliable, it will lack the Lord's light, and it will not be something that we should receive.

Enduring Sufferings

1. "Though the Lord has given you / ...adversity... oppression, / ...your eyes will see your Teacher. / And your ears will hear a word behind you, saying, / This is the way, walk in it, / When you turn to the right or turn to the left" (Isa. 30:20-21).

Adversity and oppression often cause us to be taught by the Lord so that we may know whether we are walking in the way of the Lord when we turn right or left. Many times comfort and peace can confuse us.

Obeying the Lord's Leading concerning the First Step

1. "Arise...flee into Egypt, and stay there until I tell you" (Matt. 2:13).

The Lord wanted Joseph to flee into Egypt and stay there until He told him differently. Joseph had to obey the Lord's leading in this first step and flee into Egypt before he could be led in a second step to know where the Lord wanted him to go. Similarly, when Abraham was called, the Lord led him only concerning his first step to leave the land of his fathers. After he obeyed, the Lord led him with a second step by showing him where he should live. The Lord often leads us one step at a time. When we obey, He tells us about the next step. The Lord rarely leads us two or more steps at once. Thus, we must obey the Lord's leading concerning the first step before we can receive the Lord's leading concerning the second step.

THE RESULTS OF BEING LED

Being Filled and Resting

1. "He makes me lie down in green pastures; / He leads me beside waters of rest" (Psa. 23:2; see also S. S. 1:7).

When the Lord leads us, He shepherds us, causing us to enjoy the filling of green pastures and the rest by the waters of rest.

Walking in the Paths of Righteousness

1. "He guides me on the paths of righteousness" (Psa. 23:3).

The Lord considers the paths of those who are led by Him to be righteous. Therefore, walking on the paths of righteousness is a result of being led by the Lord.

CHAPTER TWENTY-SIX

DOING THE WILL OF GOD

I. The meaning of doing God's will:
   A. Accomplishing the will of God.
   B. Taking the Lord's yoke.
   C. Keeping the Lord's commandments.
II. How to understand the will of God:
   A. Having the desire to understand.
   B. Being consecrated.
   C. Not being fashioned according to the age.
   D. Being renewed in our mind.
   E. Proving the will of God.
   F. Having a heart to do the will of God.
   G. Walking with God.
   H. Listening to the Lord's word.
   I. Rejecting the views and words of the self.
   J. Using spiritual wisdom and understanding.
III. The rewards for doing the will of God:
   A. Obtaining the top blessing.
   B. Becoming the Lord's relatives.
   C. Gaining the Lord's manifestation.
   D. Pleasing God.
   E. Entering the kingdom of the heavens.
   F. Abiding forever.
IV. The punishment for not doing the will of God:
   A. Losing the kingship.
   B. Receiving many lashes.
   C. Being refused entrance to the kingdom of the heavens by the Lord.

The points that we have examined in this volume can be combined into several sets. Chapters 17 through 20 cover four outward things that we should practice after being saved: baptism, the laying on of hands, head covering, and the breaking of bread. Chapters 21 and 22 cover two inward matters that we should pay attention to after being saved: obeying the sense of life and living in the fellowship of life. Chapters 23 through this chapter cover four things that we must practice if we want to live for the Lord: consecration, dealing with sin, being led by the Lord, and doing the will of God. If we want to live for God, we must do the will of God. If we want to do the will of God, we must be led. If we want to be led, we must consecrate and deal with sin. In application, consecration and dealing with sin are interchangeable in order. Some consecrate first and then deal with sin; some deal with sin and then consecrate. In either case one matter initiates and brings in the other. Consecration causes us to deal with sin, and dealing with sin causes us to consecrate. The more we consecrate, the more we will deal with sin, and the more we deal with sin, the more we will consecrate. A person who is consecrated to God sees his sins and deals with them one by one, and a person who deals with sins is certainly a consecrated one. These two matters have a mutual cause-and-effect relationship. We must practice these two items and practice them adequately in order to be led by the Lord. We must consecrate ourselves to God, turn our whole heart to God, and completely deal with every aspect of sin, lawlessness, and unrighteousness, clearing away the covering barriers, before we can be enlightened in the light of God's face and be led. If we can be led by God, we can do the will of God. Therefore, consecration, dealing with sin, being led, and doing the will of God are all connected.

THE MEANING OF DOING GOD'S WILL

Accomplishing the Will of God

1. "I do not seek My own will but the will of Him who sent Me" (John 5:30).

Doing the will of God means to not seek, follow, or accomplish our own will but to only seek, follow, and accomplish

God's will. People often say that they have prayed and that they are clear that the will of God is for them to go to a certain place or for them to do a certain thing. Some say that it is God's will for them to run a business. Some say that it is God's will for them to get married. But is this reliable? Is the one who thinks that he is acting according to God's will consecrated to God, and is he living for God? Is he truly not seeking, following, or accomplishing his own will but seeking, following, and accomplishing God's will? This is not a small matter. Many who claim to be acting according to the will of God are not truly practicing the will of God, because they have not consecrated themselves to Him to live for His will. They still hold on to themselves, keep things in their own hands, and live according to their own will.

A person who truly does the will of God does not seek his own will. He only seeks the will of God. This was the Lord Jesus' pattern when He was on earth as a man. In all of human history, only Jesus the Nazarene sought only the will of God and not His own will. Although He was one with God and equal to God, He willingly came to earth and stood in the position of one who was sent to do the will of God. In all things He only sought the will of Him who sent Him; He did not seek His own will. This is the meaning of doing the will of God.

2. "'Behold, I have come (in the roll of the book it is written concerning Me) to do Your will, O God'" (Heb. 10:7).

When He came to earth, the Lord spoke the words in this verse to God. This shows that the Lord did the will of God according to what was written in the Scriptures. Consequently, we should realize that any practice of the will of God must be according to the Word of God, the Bible. The Bible reveals the entire will of God in all its aspects. Whatever He wants to complete in us, whatever He wants us to do, and how He wants us to do it are revealed, in principle, in the Bible. If we truly want to do the will of God, if we truly want to seek His will, we must know the Bible and consider what the Word of God says concerning every matter. We must find God's will, in principle, concerning every matter from the Bible. Those

who want to do the will of God and act according to God's will
cannot be sloppy with the Bible but must spend a considerable amount of time to read it carefully.

If we want to do the will of God, we cannot simply do what
we think is the will of God. We cannot simply pray a few
times and say with certainty that this or that is the will of
God. Such a way is not reliable and is quite dangerous.
We often are easily deceived by our own opinions and captured by our own thoughts and views. We must bring our
opinions, thoughts, and views before the Bible and let them
be judged by the Word of God. Whoever is not willing to let his
"in my opinion," "I think," and "to my point of view" be conquered by the Word of God cannot do the will of God. We must
put our own things aside in everything and see what the
Word of God says and commands. In some things God tells us
His will in detail; in others He reveals it only in principle. For
example, the Word of God contains a great principle that
believers should not be dissimilarly yoked with unbelievers.
Consequently, we can know the will of God in many things
related to this principle. In marriage, we know that a believing brother should not marry an unbelieving woman, and a
believing sister should not be given in marriage to an unbelieving man. If we practice according to God's Word, we will
be able to practice the will of God.

3. "Not My will, but Yours be done" (Luke 22:42).

In the garden of Gethsemane, the Lord prayed these words
as He was about to be betrayed and killed. He prayed that He
would accomplish God's will, not His own will. The Lord's
prayer tells us what it means to do the will of God. To do the
will of God is to do God's will, not our own will. After the Lord
prayed this three times, He clearly knew that God's will was
for Him to die on the cross. Therefore, He willingly obeyed.
Whether or not we suffer, die for the Lord, or are even martyred, it should be according to the will of God, not our own
preference or enthusiasm. Enthusiastically volunteering to
suffer and to be martyred for the Lord cannot replace the will
of God, nor is it necessarily God's will. Anything that is
according to the predisposition and pleasure of the self
cannot be regarded as the will of God. When the Lord clearly

knew that God's will included His death, He was willing to drink the cup which the Father gave Him.

4. "The cup which the Father has given Me, shall I not drink it?" (John 18:11).

The cup of the Father in this verse refers to the Lord's death on the cross, including all of its suffering. Since God had given a cup to Him, the Lord said that He could not refuse to drink it. This tells us that the Lord's death was not according to His preference, although He willingly accepted it. The cup given to Him by God was the portion God measured to Him. By accepting the cup, He accomplished the will of God and did the will of God. The Lord's death is the highest example of doing the will of God. It shows that the criterion for doing the will of God is not doing good things but accepting what God has measured to us. God has not necessarily measured many good things for us to do; consequently, good things should not be considered as the will of God. Even preaching the gospel, casting out demons, and works of power should not be counted as the will of God if God has not measured them to us. We should not think that good or even spiritual things are automatically the will of God. These things cannot replace the will of God. While the will of God is good and spiritual, good or spiritual things are not necessarily the will of God. The will of God can only be what God has particularly measured to us. Anything that is good and spiritual must be measured to us to do; it must be assigned to us by God in order for it to be God's will for us. Even our love for the brothers should be according to God's assignment and God's measure; otherwise, it may be excessive. Only God's measure and appointment for us are the will of God. When we do what He has measured and appointed, we are doing the will of God.

One who follows the Lord certainly must deal with sin and do away with all lawlessness and unrighteousness. However, doing lawful, righteous acts is not necessarily doing the will of God. We must do what God wants us to do and what He measures for us to do in order for it to be considered as doing the will of God. When we first begin to follow the Lord and desire to please Him, our standard is typically what we consider to be good, but slowly the Lord shows us that we need to take God as our standard. The Lord wants us to be His slaves, receiving His direction and not deciding anything according to our opinion or others' perceptions. As long as something is according to the Lord's desire, we should do it even if we as well as others may think that it is wrong. This is doing the will of God. On Mount Sinai, God ordered the Levites to kill their brothers. From the human viewpoint, this seems wrong, but God wanted them to do it. When they did as God directed, they were doing the will of God, and they pleased God. In doing God's will, God is the only standard, and His intention is the only rule. Neither goodness nor morality is the criterion. Neither our own preference nor human view is the deciding factor. We should not live under man's evaluation or be influenced by man but live under God's enlightenment and governance.

5. "Setting your mind on the things of God...let him deny himself and take up his cross and follow Me" (Matt. 16:23-24).

To follow the Lord is to set our mind on the things of God. According to what the Lord said in these verses, the requirements for setting our mind on the things of God are to deny our self and take up our cross. Verse 25 shows that denying our self and losing our soul-life are absolutely related to one another. The self is the soul or soul-life. The important components of our soul are the mind, the will, and the emotion. The soul has the functions of thinking, willing, and feeling. Therefore, to deny the self is to deny the things of the soul. This is to deny our own thoughts, that is, our own views; to deny our own will, that is, our own decisions; and to deny our own emotion, that is, our own likes and dislikes. We must deny and reject whatever is of our own thought, view, will, decision, predisposition, and likes in order to set our mind on the things of God and to follow the Lord and do the will of God.

The Lord spoke this word after He told the disciples that He was going to Jerusalem to die. After hearing the Lord's word, Peter exhorted Him, saying, "God be merciful to You, Lord! This shall by no means happen to You!" (v. 22). Then the Lord said to Peter, "Get behind Me, Satan! You are a stumbling block to Me, for you are not setting your mind on the things of God, but on the things of men" (v. 23). Peter's human concern and love for the Lord had an element of Satan in them. Satan can cause people to love the Lord from their self, which keeps them from setting their mind on the things of God. Instead, he causes them to set their mind on the things of man. Satan does not cause people to do the will of God; he causes them to do their own will. Satan uses good things to influence and enter into people's opinions, and then he stirs up the self to cause the self to be active to hinder the will of God. This is the reason that the Lord spoke of denying our self, giving up our self, and denying our own will, especially in good matters. Good things are opposed to the will of God. They serve only as a means for a display of our self and our will. Satan uses good things to ruin God's will. Therefore, if we want to do the will of God, we must guard against our self, that is, our views and our intention to do good.

Many think that taking up the cross means to suffer or to suffer for the Lord. However, to suffer—even to suffer for the Lord—is not necessarily to set our mind on the things of God or to do the will of God. Suffering—especially suffering for the Lord—can sometimes be according to our own will, preference, or choice and thus is not the will of God. If it is not what God has ordained for us or what God has measured to us, it comes from our self. To truly take up the cross is to set our mind on the things of God and to do the will of God. The will of God always kills our self-life. Therefore, taking up the cross is not about suffering but about denying the self. It is not about causing the self to suffer but about putting the self in the position of death, because the goal of the cross is death, not suffering. When the Lord was crucified, we were crucified with Him on the cross. Now we need to not only confess this death but to remain in the death of the cross. Through the death of the cross, we can stand in the position of death to deny everything of the self, including our will, view, preference, and choice. This is the taking up of our cross. When we take up the cross, we follow the Lord, set our mind on the things of God, and do the will of God.

Taking the Lord's Yoke

1. "Take My yoke" (Matt. 11:29).

When an ox plows the earth, a wooden harness is placed on its neck to make it submit to its master's hand and to bear a burden. This wooden harness is called a yoke. A person consecrated to God who does the will of God under the Lord's hand is bearing the Lord's yoke. According to the Lord's regulation, the Lord's commission requires submission and the bearing of burden. Although it requires submission and the bearing of burden, the Lord promises that His yoke is easy and light.

Keeping the Lord's Commandments

1. "He who has My commandments and keeps them, he is the one who loves Me" (John 14:21, see also v. 23).

The Lord's commandments—the Bible—are the revelation of God's will. It is the embodiment of the will of God and cannot be separated from the will of God. If we keep the Lord's commandments, we will practice the will of God. Those who practice the will of God keep the Lord's commandments, and those who keep the Lord's commandments practice the will of God. These two things are one.

HOW TO UNDERSTAND THE WILL OF GOD

Having the Desire to Understand

1. "Do not be foolish, but understand what the will of the Lord is" (Eph. 5:17).

In order to understand the will of God, we must have a desire to understand. The will of God can be understood only by those who have a heart to understand. Those who do not have such a heart will never understand. Understanding begins with a desire in our heart.

One of God's commandments is to "understand what the will of the Lord is." If we do not want to understand the will of the Lord, we are disobeying the commandment of God. "Do not be foolish" is also a commandment. A saved person should be clear, but today few are clear and most are foolish. This is because most do not want to understand. God is waiting, longing for us to understand His will. If we have the desire to understand, He will enable us to understand.

Being Consecrated

1. "Present your bodies a living sacrifice" (Rom. 12:1).

The Bible speaks most clearly about how to understand the will of God in Romans 12. The first matter in verse 1 is consecration, which is a basic requirement for understanding the will of God. Consecration is a gate that we must pass through before we can understand God's will. An unconsecrated person can never understand the will of God. How can a person who has never passed though the gate understand the will of God on the other side of the gate? If we want to understand the will of God, we must consecrate. The level of earnestness and the thoroughness of our consecration has a great impact on the depth and ease of our understanding.

Not Being Fashioned according to the Age

1. "Do not be fashioned according to this age" (Rom. 12:2).

If we want to understand the will of God, we must not be fashioned according to this age. *Age* is translated as "world" in the Chinese Bible. The Greek word for *world* is *kosmos,* but the Greek word in verse 2 is *aion,* which is translated "age." *This age* is equivalent to people's understanding of the word *modern;* hence, it can also be translated as "fashionable." The world is Satan's entire organization, including its systems and institutions, which systematize the lives of everyone so that they cannot love God but instead will become enemies of God (1 John 2:15; James 4:4). An age is a part of the world; it is one section of the world that appears before us. The world is big and wide, but we are always in touch with a part of it. A section of the world appears before us, and this part or section of the world is the age, which is composed of modern and fashionable things, which oppose the will of God and cause people to be unable to understand, receive, or keep God's will. Thus, if we want to understand the will of God, we must not be fashioned according to this age, which is the part of the world that is manifested before us.

Be fashioned in Greek means "to be conformed," or "to be assimilated." Therefore, not being fashioned according to this age means not being conformed to this age, not being assimilated by this age. This is the same as not following the fashion of this age. If we want to understand the will of God, we must fulfill this requirement.

Being Renewed in Our Mind

1. "Be transformed by the renewing of the mind" (Rom. 12:2).

The renewing of the mind is another requirement for understanding God's will. The mind is our thinking faculty. Our mind is fallen and deeply contaminated by sin, the world, human emotions, and customs. It is filled with worldly thoughts and human concepts, and it cannot understand God or the will of God. Therefore, it must be renewed. All of its old thoughts, concepts, perceptions, and views must be eliminated, and it must be taught anew by God. This is what the Holy Spirit wants to do through the Bible, but we must desire to have the Holy Spirit renew our mind in this way. If we are willing, the Holy Spirit will lead us to read God's Word—the Bible—and use its teachings to kill our old thoughts and wipe out our fallen concepts by renewing our mind so that we can understand the will of God.

Although God reveals His will in our spirit through His Spirit by giving us a sense in our spirit, we must use our mind to understand the sense in our spirit. The spirit is our innermost part. Our mind surrounds our spirit. If our mind is not renewed, it cannot understand or perceive the sense of the Holy Spirit in our spirit. An unrenewed mind can be compared to a lampshade that is painted a dark color that prevents the light of the bulb from shining out. Even when a little light shines out, the light is not according to its original color. The light is so deeply covered and influenced by the dark shade that it loses its original color. The sense in our spirit is similarly influenced if our mind is not renewed. Although we have the capacity to understand, we will understand incorrectly. This is similar to wearing colored eyeglasses which change the true color of an object. If our mind is not renewed and if we cannot shake off our old thoughts and concepts, we will not be able to understand the will of God. Even if we have some understanding, our understanding will not be correct. Thus, we will be unable to perceive the original appearance of the will of God.

Proving the Will of God

1. "That you may prove what the will of God is, that which is good and well pleasing and perfect" (Rom. 12:2).

Understanding the will of God involves proving. To prove is to search for the good, well pleasing, and perfect will of God in everything. In order to prove the will of God, we need to stand in a position of consecration, to not follow the age of the world, to be renewed in our mind according to the Word of God, the Bible, and to understand the sense in our spirit and the condition of our environment. Searching out God's will in everything involves discerning the motive, goal, and nature of things. Therefore, we must stand on God's side in the reality of our consecration, be absolutely outside this age, and see God's view according to a mind that has been renewed and taught by God. We must always use the clear teachings, principles, and examples of the Bible to measure and prove the will of God and to see whether or not our ways are one with the will of God. We must use the sense in our spirit to test and judge what is according to the will of God. We also should consider whether or not the environment confirms what we have realized. If we are willing to prove the will of God in this manner, it will not be difficult for us to understand the will of God.

Having a Heart to Do the Will of God

1. "If anyone resolves to do His will, he will know" (John 7:17).

If anyone resolves—has a heart—to do God's will, he will know God's will. If we want to understand the will of God, we must not only have a heart to understand but also a heart to do His will. God is not willing to reveal His will to those who do not have the heart to understand, nor does He want to reveal His will to those who have the heart to understand but not a heart to do it. Only those who have the heart to both understand and do the will of God can gain a revelation of God's will from Him. Therefore, we must resolve to do God's will if we want to understand the will of God.

Walking with God

1. **"Abraham walked with them to send them away. And Jehovah said, Shall I hide from Abraham what I am about to do?"** (Gen. 18:16-17).

A heart to understand and prove the will of God and even the resolve to do the will of God are not enough; we must spend time before God. We must walk with God. God once visited Abraham with two angels. God told him about many things, but He did not tell him about His decision to destroy Sodom and Gomorrah and to save Lot. It was only when Abraham went with God and the angels to bring them on their way that God finally told Abraham of His will. He said, "Shall I hide from Abraham what I am about to do?" (v. 17). If Abraham had not gone with God to bring Him on His way, God's will would have remained hidden from him. Abraham's going with God to bring Him on His way caused God to open to Abraham to let him know what was hidden in His heart. This is similar to when a person goes to a friend's house and converses with him for quite a while but is unwilling to tell him the true reason until it is time to say goodbye. The friend accompanies him to the gate and, not wanting to leave him, goes with him for a while to bring him on his way. Then the visitor usually tells his friend what is really on his heart. We usually tell what is on our heart only to friends with whom we have a close, affectionate friendship. This is the situation of Genesis 18; Abraham was a friend of God, and they had a close, affectionate friendship. Consequently, God opened to Abraham and spoke what was on His heart to him. This shows that we must walk with God and have a close, affectionate friendship with God to know and understand His will.

Listening to the Lord's Word

1. "Sat at the Lord's feet and was listening to His word" (Luke 10:39).

If we want to understand the Lord's word, there must be a close, affectionate friendship between us and God. We must also learn to listen to the Lord's word. Mary not only sat at the Lord's feet but also listened to His word. The Lord's will is often expressed through His word. Thus, if we want to know how to understand the Lord's will, we must let Him speak and we must listen to His speaking. When Abraham was fellowshipping with God, he let God finish speaking (Gen. 18:33). He listened to God until God finished speaking, so he clearly and thoroughly understood the will of God. Often we do not allow the Lord to speak, and we do not listen to Him in our fellowship with Him. Even when we let the Lord speak and we listen to Him, we often do not allow Him to finish speaking and we do not listen until He has finished. Therefore, it is difficult to clearly know the will of God. Mary sat at the Lord's feet, but she was not like us. She allowed the Lord to speak, and she listened to Him. She also allowed the Lord to finish speaking, and she listened until He was finished. Therefore, she understood the Lord's prophetic revelation of His death and poured pure ointment on Him ahead of time, which He praised. The other disciples could not understand the Lord's will concerning His death, because they did not listen to the Lord in this way. Listening to the Lord's word is absolutely necessary to understanding the will of God.

Rejecting the Views and Words of the Self

1. "Who is this who darkens counsel / By words without knowledge?" (Job 38:2).

If we want to understand the will of God, we must reject our own views and words. These darken the will of God and are often used by Satan to hinder the will of God. When we seek the will of God by listening to His word, we must reject the views and words of the self. Job's own view and words only darkened God's will to him. When he finally rejected his own views and stopped speaking his own words, he knew and understood the will of God.

Using Spiritual Wisdom and Understanding

1. "That you may be filled with the full knowledge of His will in all spiritual wisdom and understanding" (Col. 1:9).

Finally, if we want to understand God's will, we must have and use spiritual wisdom and understanding. Wisdom refers to the knowledge in our spirit that causes us to have an extraordinary seeing of the will of God. Understanding refers to the understanding in our mind that allows us to ordinarily understand God's will. Wisdom is in our spirit, so it is spiritual. Although understanding is in our mind, it should also be spiritual. This requires that our mind be renewed by the Holy Spirit and be full of the Holy Spirit's enlightenment and inspiration. We must have and use such wisdom and understanding to understand the will of God. We must ask God for this wisdom (James 1:5). We must beg God to give us the power to understand and to open the eyes of our heart. We also need to earnestly deal with our spirit and heart so that everything unclean and unrighteous in our spirit and heart is removed, making our spirit upright and bright and our mind fresh and clean. Furthermore, we need to exercise, that is, to practice using our spirit and our renewed mind. Then our spirit will have wisdom from God, and our mind will have spiritual understanding so that we can know and understand the will of God.

THE REWARDS FOR DOING THE WILL OF GOD

The rewards for doing the will of God are many and great. Therefore, it is important to do the will of God.

Obtaining the Top Blessing

1. "But there is need of one thing, for Mary has chosen the good part, which shall not be taken away from her" (Luke 10:42).

Mary acted according to the Lord's heart's desire, so there

was need of only one thing. She gained the good part, which could not be taken away from her.

2. "He said, Blessed rather are those who hear the word of God and keep it" (Luke 11:28).

When someone spoke of the person who bore the Lord Jesus as being blessed, He answered, "Blessed rather are those who hear the word of God and keep it," that is, those who do the will of God. This shows that the blessing for doing the will of God is even greater than the blessing that Mary received in bearing the Lord Jesus.

Becoming the Lord's Relatives

1. "Whoever does the will of My Father who is in the heavens, he is My brother and sister and mother" (Matt. 12:50).

Some people think that being a relative of the Lord in the flesh would be a great blessing, but the Lord said that whoever does the will of God is His relative. By practicing the will of God, we can receive such a sweet, blessed reward.

Gaining the Lord's Manifestation

1. "He who has My commandments and keeps them, he is the one who loves Me; and he who loves Me will be loved by My Father, and I will love Him and will manifest Myself to him...and make an abode with him" (John 14:21, 23).

Keeping the Lord's commandments because we love the Lord is doing the will of God. According to the Lord's promise here, we can gain the love and the manifestation, the presence, of the Lord and the Father. What can be sweeter than the love of the Lord and the Father? What can be more precious than the manifestation of the Lord and the Father? These blessings, which are promised by the Lord to those who love Him and keep His commandments, cannot be surpassed. If we want to practically enjoy the love of the Lord and the Father and if we want to personally experience the manifestation, the presence, of the Lord and the Father, we must love the Lord and keep His commandments.

Pleasing God

1. "Samuel said, Does Jehovah delight in burnt offerings and sacrifices / As much as in obeying the voice of Jehovah? / Behold, to obey is better than sacrifice, / And to heed, than the fat of rams" (1 Sam. 15:22).

Pleasing God is a great blessing. Many think that they can please God by offering something to Him. But this verse says that God has more delight in our obedience to the voice of the Lord than in any sacrifice we could offer. To obey His voice is to practice the will of God. In the Lord's eyes, obeying and hearkening are better than offering sacrifices. Therefore, the Lord is more pleased by those who listen to His commandments and do His will.

Entering the Kingdom of the Heavens

1. "Not everyone who says to Me, Lord, Lord, will enter into the kingdom of the heavens, but he who does the will of My Father who is in the heavens" (Matt. 7:21).

Entering into the kingdom of the heavens is different from being saved. Being saved is a matter of grace, which we obtain by believing. Entering into the kingdom of the heavens is a matter of reward, which is gained by doing the will of God. Whoever calls on the name of the Lord shall be saved, but not everyone can enter into the kingdom of the heavens. We do not enter the kingdom of the heavens merely by calling on the Lord's name. If we want to enter the kingdom of the heavens, we must do the will of God. The kingdom of the heavens is the reward that God has prepared for those who do His will.

Abiding Forever

1. "The world is passing away, and its lust, but he who does the will of God abides forever" (1 John 2:17).

The world is the enemy of God, and its lust opposes the will of God; therefore, the world and its lust will pass away. God and His will are eternal; therefore, those who do His will also abide forever. Whatever we have of the world and its lust will pass away. Whatever we have of God and His will abides forever. Just as passing away is the punishment for loving the world and following its lust, abiding forever is the reward for loving God and doing His will.

THE PUNISHMENT FOR NOT DOING THE WILL OF GOD

There is a reward for doing the will of God and a punishment for not doing the will of God. Many believers think that there are only rewards as an encouragement for doing His will but that there are no consequences as a punishment for not doing His will, because God always deals with us in grace and love. This thought is wrong. In God's Word, the Bible, we are told that those who do the will of God receive a reward, and we are also told that those who do not do the will of God receive a punishment. Furthermore, the punishment for not doing the will of God is as heavy as the reward for doing the will of God is great.

Losing the Kingship

1. **"Rebellion is like the sin of divination, / And insubordination is like idolatry and teraphim. / Because you have rejected the word of Jehovah, / He has also rejected you from being king"** (1 Sam. 15:23).

God commanded Saul to utterly destroy the Amalekites and all their animals. But Saul did not listen to God's commandment; he destroyed only what was bad and kept what was good. Because Saul rejected the word of the Lord (which is the same as not doing the will of God), God rejected him from being king, causing him to lose the kingship. In God's eyes the sin of rebellion is as the sin of divination, and insubordination is as idolatry and teraphim. This should be such a warning to us. If we do not do the will of God today, we will lose the blessing of being kings with the Lord in the future.

Receiving Many Lashes

1. **"That slave who knew his master's will and did not prepare or do according to his will, will receive many lashes"** (Luke 12:47).

If we know the Lord's will but do not do it, we will receive many lashes when the Lord returns.

Being Refused Entrance
to the Kingdom of the Heavens by the Lord

1. "**Many will say to Me in that day, Lord, Lord, was it not in Your name that we prophesied, and in Your name cast out demons, and in Your name did many works of power? And then I will declare to them: I never knew you. Depart from Me, you workers of lawlessness**" (Matt. 7:22-23).

In these verses the Lord said that in the future many—not just a few—who call Him Lord will be refused entrance into the kingdom of the heavens because they did not do the will of God. These are saved ones, since they call on the Lord's name. Although they preach, cast out demons, and do many works of power in the Lord's name, they do not do them in accordance with God's will and are workers of lawlessness in the Lord's eyes. Workers of lawlessness are those who are disobedient. What they do may be good and spiritual, but they do not do it according to God's rule; therefore, it is lawlessness. This is like a student who studies after ten o'clock in the evening, even though the school has a rule that all lights must be out after that time. Although his studying is good, he is breaking school rules. Because of this type of lawlessness, the Lord will disapprove of many, and He will not allow them to enter the kingdom of the heavens. If we do not do the will of God today and gain the Lord's approval, the Lord will refuse us entrance into His kingdom as a punishment in the future.

ABOUT THE AUTHOR

Witness Lee was born in 1905 in northern China and raised in a Christian family. At age 19 he was fully captured for Christ and immediately consecrated himself to preach the gospel for the rest of his life. Early in his service, he met Watchman Nee, a renowned preacher, teacher, and writer. Witness Lee labored together with Watchman Nee under his direction. In 1934 Watchman Nee entrusted Witness Lee with the responsibility for his publication operation, called the Shanghai Gospel Bookroom.

Prior to the Communist takeover in 1949, Witness Lee was sent by Watchman Nee and his other co-workers to Taiwan to ensure that the things delivered to them by the Lord would not be lost. Watchman Nee instructed Witness Lee to continue the former's publishing operation abroad as the Taiwan Gospel Bookroom, which has been publicly recognized as the publisher of Watchman Nee's works outside China. Witness Lee's work in Taiwan manifested the Lord's abundant blessing. From a mere 350 believers, newly fled from the mainland, the churches in Taiwan grew to 20,000 in five years.

In 1962 Witness Lee felt led of the Lord to come to the United States, and he began to minister in Los Angeles. During his 35 years of service in the U.S., he ministered in weekly meetings and weekend conferences, delivering several thousand spoken messages. Much of his speaking has since been published as over 400 titles. Many of these have been translated into over fourteen languages. He gave his last public conference in February 1997 at the age of 91.

He leaves behind a prolific presentation of the truth in the Bible. His major work, *Life-study of the Bible*, comprises over 25,000 pages of commentary on every book of the Bible from the perspective of the believers' enjoyment and experience of God's divine life in Christ through the Holy Spirit. Witness Lee was the chief editor of a new translation of the New Testament into Chinese called the Recovery Version and directed the translation of the same into English. The Recovery Version also appears in a number of other languages. He provided an extensive body of footnotes, outlines, and spiritual cross references. A radio broadcast of his messages can be heard on Christian radio stations in the United States. In 1965 Witness Lee founded Living Stream Ministry, a non-profit corporation, located in Anaheim, California, which officially presents his and Watchman Nee's ministry.

Witness Lee's ministry emphasizes the experience of Christ as life and the practical oneness of the believers as the Body of Christ. Stressing the importance of attending to both these matters, he led the churches under his care to grow in Christian life and function. He was unbending in his conviction that God's goal is not narrow sectarianism but the Body of Christ. In time, believers began to meet simply as the church in their localities in response to this conviction. In recent years a number of new churches have been raised up in Russia and in many European countries.

OTHER BOOKS PUBLISHED BY
Living Stream Ministry

Titles by Witness Lee:

Abraham—Called by God	978-0-7363-0359-0
The Experience of Life	978-0-87083-417-2
The Knowledge of Life	978-0-87083-419-6
The Tree of Life	978-0-87083-300-7
The Economy of God	978-0-87083-415-8
The Divine Economy	978-0-87083-268-0
God's New Testament Economy	978-0-87083-199-7
The World Situation and God's Move	978-0-87083-092-1
Christ vs. Religion	978-0-87083-010-5
The All-inclusive Christ	978-0-87083-020-4
Gospel Outlines	978-0-87083-039-6
Character	978-0-87083-322-9
The Secret of Experiencing Christ	978-0-87083-227-7
The Life and Way for the Practice of the Church Life	978-0-87083-785-2
The Basic Revelation in the Holy Scriptures	978-0-87083-105-8
The Crucial Revelation of Life in the Scriptures	978-0-87083-372-4
The Spirit with Our Spirit	978-0-87083-798-2
Christ as the Reality	978-0-87083-047-1
The Central Line of the Divine Revelation	978-0-87083-960-3
The Full Knowledge of the Word of God	978-0-87083-289-5
Watchman Nee—A Seer of the Divine Revelation ...	978-0-87083-625-1

Titles by Watchman Nee:

How to Study the Bible	978-0-7363-0407-8
God's Overcomers	978-0-7363-0433-7
The New Covenant	978-0-7363-0088-9
The Spiritual Man • 3 volumes	978-0-7363-0269-2
Authority and Submission	978-0-7363-0185-5
The Overcoming Life	978-1-57593-817-2
The Glorious Church	978-0-87083-745-6
The Prayer Ministry of the Church	978-0-87083-860-6
The Breaking of the Outer Man and the Release ...	978-1-57593-955-1
The Mystery of Christ	978-1-57593-954-4
The God of Abraham, Isaac, and Jacob	978-0-87083-932-0
The Song of Songs	978-0-87083-872-9
The Gospel of God • 2 volumes	978-1-57593-953-7
The Normal Christian Church Life	978-0-87083-027-3
The Character of the Lord's Worker	978-1-57593-322-1
The Normal Christian Faith	978-0-87083-748-7
Watchman Nee's Testimony	978-0-87083-051-8

Available at
Christian bookstores, or contact Living Stream Ministry
2431 W. La Palma Ave. • Anaheim, CA 92801
1-800-549-5164 • www.livingstream.com